D1521294

The Earth's Fragile Systems

IFIAS Research Series

Vol. 1. G. Hallsworth, *The Anatomy, Physiology and Psychology of Erosion*, John Wiley and Sons Ltd., Chichester, 1987.

Vol. 2. Rob Koudstaal, *Water Quality Management Plan, North Sea: Framework for Analysis*, A. A. Balkema, Rotterdam, 1987, Coastal Waters No. 1.

Vol. 3. Lies Dekker, Blair T. Bower & Rob Koudstaal, *Management of Toxic Materials in an International Setting, A Case Study of Cadmium in the North Sea*, A. A. Balkema, Rotterdam, 1987, Coastal Waters No. 2.

Vol. 4. Thorkil Kristensen and Johan Peter Paludan, *The Earth's Fragile Systems: Perspectives on Global Change*, Westview Press, Boulder, 1988.

Published in cooperation with
The International Federation of
Institutes for Advanced Study (IFIAS)

The Earth's Fragile Systems

Perspectives on Global Change

EDITED BY

Thorkil Kristensen
and Johan Peter Paludan

Westview Press
BOULDER & LONDON

IFIAS Research Series

Copyright © 1988 by the International Federation of Institutes for Advanced Studies

Published in 1988 in the United States of America by Westview Press, Inc., 5500 Central Avenue, Boulder, Colorado 80301

Library of Congress Cataloging-in-Publication Data
The Earth's fragile systems.
  (IFIAS research series; #4)
  1. Ecology.   2. Environmental protection.
3. Man—Influence on nature.   4. Conservation of
natural resources.   I. Kristensen, Thorkil, 1899-
II. Paludan, Johan Peter.   III. Series.
QH541.E27   1988   304.2   88-5692
ISBN O-8133-7486-3

Printed and bound in the United States of America

The paper used in this publication meets the requirements of the American National Standard for Permanence of Paper for Printed Library Materials Z39.48-1984.

10   9   8   7   6   5   4   3   2   1

Contents

Contributors

Sir Hermann Bondi, Churchill College, Oxford University; Chairman, IFIAS, Toronto, Canada

F. William Burley, World Resources Institute, Washington, D.C.

Ian Burton, IFIAS, Toronto, and the University of Toronto, Canada

Bent Elbek, Niels Bohr Institute, University of Copenhagen, Denmark

John W. Firor, National Center for Atmospheric Research, Boulder, Colorado

Peter T. Hazlewood, World Resources Institute, Washington, D.C.

Prof. Dr. E. El-Hinnawi, National Research Center, Cairo, Egypt

Thorkil Kristensen, Institute for Futures Studies, Copenhagen, Denmark

Johan Peter Paludan, Institute for Futures Studies, Copenhagen, Denmark

Amos Richmond, The Miles and Lillian Cahn Chair in Economic Botany, The Jacob Blaustein Institute for Desert Research, Ben Gurion University of the Negev, Sede-Boquer, Israel

Don Scott-Kemmis, Centre for Technology & Social Change, The University of Wollongong, Australia

Malcolm Slesser, Resource Use Institute, Scotland

Dr. Pamela Stokes, Institute for Environmental Studies, Canada

Foreword

This slim volume was prepared by IFIAS, the International Federation of Institutes for Advanced Study. It is concerned with some of the most pressing and worrying of the problems afflicting our globe, problems that have been discussed in various forums and are well known not to be simple intellectually, practically or politically. However, what is presented here is characteristic of the workings of IFIAS, with contributions from member institutes in industrialized and in developing countries, with individuals having views and laying them open to discussion by others in the Federation. It is these comments, as much as the papers, that serve to underline the spread of views, a spread that needs to be narrowed down over the years before an acceptable program for action can emerge.

The purpose of this volume is, first, to expound the problems and to stress their importance and, second, to contribute significantly to the dialogues that need to be pursued so energetically in order to reach a basis from which action can be proposed in a manner that is conducive to wide acceptance, rather than to the fostering of further dissension.

In this, as in all IFIAS work, the final aim is a severely practical one – to be of real help to those who have to make major decisions. I trust that this book's contribution to this process will be appreciated and will be seen to be effective.

Sir Hermann Bondi
Chairman, IFIAS

Editors' Note

This collection of papers has been on its way for some time. The aim of this collection of papers is that IFIAS member institutes should join in the preparation of a series of essays and commentaries on recent events and trends and their likely consequences into the midterm future.

At the end of 1984 the Board of Trustees approved this idea. The Institute for Futures Studies was appointed coordinator and editor.

The coordination and editing of *The Earth's Fragile Systems: Perspectives onGlobal Change* papers have proven at the same time to be a fascinating and a frustrating task: fascinating because of the authors and their subjects; frustrating because of various practical problems in getting the collection of papers ready and in finding a publisher.

After consultation with Alexander King, Ian Burton, Jorgen Rossen and Sam Nilsson, selected persons at the IFIAS member institutes were approached. In the end this resulted in the papers here presented. These papers were sent to all IFIAS member Institutes for comments.

The comments here reproduced were received during the first half of 1986. As to be seen, some of the authors have chosen to respond to these comments.

It is the editors' contention that the timelessness of the subjects dealt with in these papers justifies their publication despite the time that has passed since their conception.

The editors would like to thank Jorgen Rossen, special advisor to IFIAS, for his editorial as well as practical assistance.

Thorkil Kristensen
Programme Coordinator

Johan Peter Paludan
Project Assistant

INSTITUTE FOR FUTURE STUDIES
Copenhagen

1

Tropical Forests: A Resource in Jeopardy

F. William Burley and Peter T. Hazlewood
World Resources Institute
Washington, D.C.

Introduction

One-fourth of humanity lives in poverty, characterized by poor health, malnutrition, chronic deprivation, and shortened lives. This suffering and wasted potential is one of the great tragedies of modern times. A contributing cause of this desperate situation is the widespread loss of forests taking place throughout the developing world. Tragically, it is the rural poor themselves who are the primary agents of destruction as they clear forests for agricultural land, fuelwood, and other necessities. Lacking other means to meet their daily survival needs, rural populations are forced to steadily undermine the capacity of the natural environment to support them.

The relationship between poverty and deforestation is clear, but it is not inevitable. Solutions to this cycle of increasing misery are already known and demonstrated. Spontaneous tree planting and grassroots conservation initiatives are beginning to gain ground. Given appropriate government policies and institutional support, much can be done now through well-designed forestry and agricultural investment programs to accelerate this process. The evidence is clear that forest conservation and development projects can earn high enough rates of economic return to be self-sustaining. The challenge is to put these solutions to work elsewhere for the millions of rural poor seeking a better future.

To meet this challenge requires political leadership. The failure of national governments and the international community to respond adequately to the deforestation crisis has led to extremely high costs in developing countries. Much of the environmental damage, decline in agricultural productivity, and human suffering that developing countries are facing today could have been reduced by greater political commitment to forest conservation and development.

Tropical forests are one of the earth's most valuable natural resources. Throughout history, they have been essential sources of food, fuel, shelter, medicines, and many other products. They sustain people and their environments by protecting soil and water resources and providing habitat for an estimated 50% of the world's plant and animal species. Although the evidence still is being debated, it is likely that tropical forests also influence regional and global climate.

The lives of more than one billion people in the developing countries, primarily the rural and urban poor, are disrupted by periodic flooding, fuelwood scarcity, degradation of soil and water resources, and reduced agricultural productivity — all caused in whole or in part by deforestation. Scientists estimate that 40% of the biologically-rich tropical moist forests have been cleared or degraded already, and in many developing countries they will nearly disappear in two or three decades if present trends continue.

In December, 1984, the World Resources Institute in cooperation with The World Bank and the United Nations Development Program, convened an international task force of nine leading experts in forestry, agriculture, and conservation. Backed by a staff and consultants, the task force produced a report,"Tropical Forests: A Call for Action," which was published and released in October, 1985. This article is a condensation of that report.

Deforestation in Developing Countries

Developed and developing countries differ sharply in the condition of their forests and the status of forest conservation and management. The forest area of many developed countries has stabilized and, in some cases, has increased during this century.

Having achieved a reasonably stable forest resource base, forest policy planners in the developed world have turned their attention to maximizing forest productivity. Well established forestry institutions now exist in most developed countries. With enough wood production to meet most of its needs for timber, plywood, and paper, the developed world maintains many forests solely for their recreational, protective, and aesthetic values.

In contrast to the developed world, forests in the developing world have declined by nearly half in this century. Forty percent of the closed tropical forests have been cleared, logged, or degraded. Most of the remaining 800 million hectares are in the Amazon and Congo basins, where they survive largely because of their vastness and relative inaccessibility.

However, even in countries such as Brazil where the national deforestation rate is relatively low, large areas of closed forests have been cleared in several parts of the country. Open forests – distinguished from closed forests by their discontinuous canopy and substantial grass layer – have also suffered extensive degradation.

Each year more than 11 million hectares of tropical forests are being cleared for other uses – 7.5 million hectares of closed forests and 3.8 million hectares of open forests. In most countries the deforestation rate is rising. If this continues, at least 225 million hectares of tropical forests will be cleared by the year 2000.

Deforestation is a complex problem. The spread of agriculture, including crop and livestock production, is the single greatest factor in forest destruction. The rural poor are often unjustly held responsible for the loss of forests. They are often the instruments of forest destruction, caught in a chain of events that force them into destructive patterns of land use to meet their basic needs for food and fuel. The true causes of deforestation are poverty, skewed land distribution (due to historical patterns of land settlement and commercial agriculture development), and low agricultural productivity.

These factors, combined with the rapid population growth, have led to increasingly severe pressure on forest lands in developed countries. As productive land becomes scarce, small farmers have been pushed into fragile upland forest areas and marginal lowlands that cannot support large numbers of people practicing subsistence agriculture. The loss of forests and rising population pressure have forced farmers to shorten fallow periods, degrading the productive capacity of the land and setting in motion a downward spiral of forest destruction. This situation prevails now in many developing countries, and it can change only if rural populations are given alternatives to this ecologically destructive way of living.

Government policies have contributed to depletion and destruction of tropical forests. Many developing countries have forest policies (such as direct subsidies and lenient forest concession terms) that encourage unsustainable use of forest resources. Similarly, agriculture, land settlement, and other nonforestry policies often lead to encroachment on forests far beyond what is economically justified or environmentally sound.

Developed countries must share the blame for the plight of forests in developing countries. Developed country demand for tropical timber has been rising steadily. For many developing countries desperate to earn foreign exchange to ease their international debt problems, forests represent a ready source of income. A related problem is the generally low price paid for tropical timber. When prices are too low to fully reflect forest management and replacement costs, there is little incentive to manage the resource for the long term. This results in the"cut-and-run" pattern of commercial forest exploitation practiced in many developing countries.

Given the history of forest use in developed countries, some ask why developing countries should not follow the same path. This is a fair question, but major differences between the two situations dictate against such a strategy. The most serious difference is human numbers. The pressure of rapidly increasing populations in most developing countries completely alters the context of forest land use.

This does not mean that forests in developing countries should be left untouched. Forests are valuable resources that can provide myriad benefits to people and support economic growth. The real issue is how these resources are managed and put to use. Forests in most areas are now being exploited in an unsustainable manner. In effect, a renewable resource is being treated as a nonrenewable resource.

Our Dependence on Forests and Trees

Almost 70% of the people in the developing countries, most of whom live in rural areas, depend mainly on wood to meet their household energy needs. Low incomes restrict their ability to buy any type of fuel, so these families use wood, crop residues, dry dung, twigs, grass, or whatever source of energy can be freely gathered.

However, the importance of forests and trees extends far beyond their value as a source of fuelwood. They provide wood for building poles, furniture, roof timbers, fencing, household implements, and many other uses.

Nonwood resources from tropical forests are also important. Trees are an essential source of fodder for livestock. They also provide fruits and nuts, honey, gums, oils, resins, medicines, tannins, fibers, and other materials. There is a growing recognition of the importance of small-scale forest-based enterprises as a source of nonfarm employment and income.

Forests and trees also contribute to agricultural production. In the tropics, trees do not necessarily compete with food crops, and they are often an integral part of farming systems. Trees can play a vital role in sustaining crop yields by:

- Helping maintain the soil and water base for agricultural production, particularly in upland watersheds, by reducing erosion and moderating stream flows
- Restoring soil fertility in shifting agriculture
- Increasing farm crop yields by 20-30% in arid and semiarid areas by slowing wind and increasing soil moisture

- Increasing soil nitrogen content through use of nitrogen-fixing tree species
- Providing a significant proportion of livestock feed requirements, especially in upland and semiarid regions.

As deforestation progresses, however, it erodes the quality of life of millions of people in developing countries. For the poorest living close to the land, survival is threatened by the loss of the vegetation upon which they depend. As trees disappear, so do their source of household energy and many other goods. Worse, a chain of events is set in motion that leads to declining food production, lower standards of living, and, in many cases, desertification.

Declining Food Production and Desertification

Deforestation is having serious impacts on food production. As fuelwood supplies are depleted, families turn to whatever substitutes are available, primarily crop residues and animal dung. Their use as fuel robs farm fields of badly needed organic matter and nutrients. The failure to renew soil fertility leads inevitably to declines in crop yields.

The annual burning of an estimated 400 million tons of dung to cook meals in areas where fuelwood is scarce decreases food grain harvests by more than 14 million tons. This loss in the food supply is nearly double the amount of food aid annually provided to developing countries.

The removal of tree cover can further reduce agricultural productivity by loss of the benefits trees provide for the farming systems. Widespread loss of vegetation reduces the effectiveness of rainfall by decreasing the amount of water that percolates into the ground. As a result, water runoff increases, erosion accelerates, the water table is lowered, and springs and wells dry up.

In its most extreme form, deforestation leads to "desertification" — a process of decline in the biological productivity of arid, semiarid, and subhumid lands (or drylands). The result is desert. Drylands are particularly sensitive to human abuse because of the fragility of the soil and low and erratic rainfall. Traditional production systems are breaking down in these areas under the combined pressures of population growth and poverty. Drylands are being stripped of woody vegetation through agricultural clearing, overcutting for fuelwood, overgrazing, and bush fires, eroding the land and accelerating the spread of deserts.

Desertification is undermining the food-producing capacity of dry regions of Africa, Asia, and Latin America. A 1984 assessment by the United Nations Environment Program shows that desertification is spreading, affecting more and more land and people. Some 1.3 billion hectares are at least moderately desertified in Africa, Asia, and Latin America, and more than 300 million people live in areas at least moderately or severely desertified. The most critical areas in terms of the number of people affected are rainfed croplands, where desertification is accelerating in all three regions. Forestry and agriculture have a vital role in preventing the spread of deserts and in recovering some of the marginal areas already abandoned.

The Fuelwood Crisis

More than 80% of the wood harvested in developing countries is used as fuelwood, compared with less than 20% in developed countries. Further, developing countries rely on forests to meet half of their total needs for energy.

In rural areas, gathering and transporting fuelwood increasingly dominates the daily lives of millions of people — 100 to 300 workdays each year must be devoted to supplying a household. Women and children shoulder most of the burden for finding and carrying home the wood needed to cook the day's meal. In Nepal, groups of villagers must leave at sunrise in order to return by sunset with a backbreaking load that will last only 3 to 4 days. The increasing time needed to collect fuelwood is disrupting family stability and shortens the time that can be devoted to weeding and tending crops, preparing food, and other domestic activities.

In urban areas, most households must buy fuelwood or charcoal. Prices have risen so sharply in recent years that in many areas the wood used for cooking costs more than the food being cooked. Between 20% and 40% of the cash income of the average urban household must be set aside to buy wood or charcoal. In some countries, malnutrition is due not to lack of food but to the lack of fuelwood for cooking. Families are forced to eat less nutritious quick-cooking foods or even uncooked meals to an extent that damages their health. Urban demand for fuelwood and charcoal is expanding the economic distances for clearing and hauling wood, leading to ever-widening circles of devastation around cities and towns.

A recent FAO analysis indicates that 1.5 billion people (70% of the 2 billion who rely on fuelwood to meet a major part of their household energy needs) are cutting wood faster than it is growing back. Some 125 million people in 23 countries cannot find enough wood to meet their needs, even by overcutting the forests.

Without major policy changes to ensure better fuelwood conservation and increased supplies, by the year 2000 some 2.4 billion people (more than half the people in the developing countries) will face fuelwood shortages and will be caught up in a destructive cycle of deforestation, fuelwood scarcity, poverty, and malnutrition.

The rising demand for fuelwood and poles, tree fodder, and agricultural land has greatly accelerated deforestation, bringing in its wake not only shortages of the most important source of household energy in the developing countries but a disastrous series of food crises.

- 63 out of 95 developing countries are faced with inadequate supplies of fuelwood. More than half of the most severely affected countries are in sub-Saharan Africa.
- 35 of the countries with fuelwood shortages have no proven oil or gas reserves, which, combined with low GNP per capita and low rates of economic growth, severely constrains their ability to switch from traditional biomass fuels to fossil fuels.
- Shortages of fuelwood are most acute in semiarid and mountain areas where the productivity of natural woodlands is lowest and the risk of over-exploitating the environment is greatest. Fuelwood deficits are increasingly common in densely settled lowlands, and in areas of rapidly growing population and agriculture.

Countries with major shortages of fuelwood

Region	Countries affected by acute scarcity of fuelwood or deficits	Other countries with areas of fuelwood deficits
Africa:	Botswana	Angola
	Burkina Faso	Benin
	Burundi	Cameroon
	Cape Verde	Congo
	Chad	Gambia
	Comoros	Guinea
	Djibouti	Madagascar
	Ethiopia	Mozambique
	Kenya	Nigeria
	Lesotho	Swaziland
	Malawi	Tanzania
	Mali	Togo
	Mauretania	Uganda
	Mauritius	Zaire
	Namibia	Zambia
	Niger	Zimbabwe
	Reunion	
	Rwanda	
	Senegal	
	Somalia	
	Sudan	

Asia:	Afghanistan	Bangladesh
	China	Indonesia (Java)
	India	Philippines
	Nepal	Sri Lanka
	Pakistan	Thailand
	Turkey	Viet Nam
Latin	El Salvador	Brazil
America:	Haiti	Costa Rica
	Bolivia (part)	Chile
	Peru	Colombia
		Cuba
		Dominican
		Republic
		Ecuador
		Guatemala
		Jamaica
		Mexico
		Trinidad and
		Tobago

Source: Based on the 1980 study by FAO of fuelwood supplies in developing countries. Fuelwood scarcity was defined as an inability to meet minimum requirements, even by over-exploitation of remaining woodlands. Fuelwood deficits indicate that demand is met by harvesting wood faster than it is being replenished.

At present rates of consumption, between the years 1980 and 2000 the annual fuelwood deficit in developing countries will grow from 407 to 925 million cubic meters. This shortfall, which is now met by overcutting forests, is equivalent to the annual output of wood from 80 million hectares of fuelwood plantations. The current rate of tree-planting in tropical countries is estimated to be 1 million hectares per year, or little more than 1% of what is required. However, official statistics on tree planting often underestimate the number of trees planted outside of government-sponsored programs.

Degraded Upland Watersheds

Upland and lowland populations within a watershed depend closely on one another. On upland hills, violent tropical rainstorms require close protection of the soil by vegetation. For this purpose, forest cover is best, but contour-planted tree crops can be effective. Annually cultivated crops expose bare soil and need full protection by terracing.

Skillful land use that maintains the environmental stability of upland source areas of streams not only benefits upland inhabitants but can also protect downstream hydropower reservoirs and irrigation systems from mud and debris. Erosion and sedimentation can be kept to natural levels, thus minimizing floods which bring damage and misery to those living below. In return, the hill populations depend on the wealth generated by the larger communities in the valley bottoms and plains for providing roads and other services.

Despite their importance, an estimated 160 million hectares of upland watersheds in the tropical developing countries have been seriously degraded. Increasing population pressures and destructive land use have resulted in the loss of fuelwood and fodder supplies, greater flood damage, intensification of drought, sedimentation of dams and reservoirs, and loss of crops and livestock. This has aggravated poverty in the hills and caused unnecessary damage to the lowlands. More than one billion people in the developing world are hurt by this process. An estimated 160 million hectares of upland watersheds have been seriously degraded in Africa, Asia, and Latin America. Countries with serious upland watershed problems are:

Africa	Asia	Latin America
Burundi	China	Argentina
Ethiopia	India	Bolivia
Guinea	Indonesia	Brazil
Kenya	Nepal	Chile
Lesotho	Pakistan	Colombia
Madagascar	Philippines	Costa Rica
Mozambique	Thailand	Ecuador
Tanzania		Guatemala
Zimbabwe		Haiti
		Jamaica
		Mexico
		Nicaragua
		Panama
		Peru

The Himalayan Range

This region contains the world's most severe watershed problems. On the lowland plains of Pakistan, India, and Bangladesh, over 400 million people are "hostage" to the land-use practices of 46 million people living in the hills. In India alone, costs of flood damage and destruction of reservoirs and irrigation systems have averaged US $1 billion a year in compensation and damage-prevention measures. There is a vast potential for generating hydroelectric power in the Himalayan region, but at present investment in reservoirs is unsound because of sedimentation.

The Andean Range

The eastern plains that adjoin the steep foothills of the Andes are typically infertile and sparsely populated, but the foothills are heavily settled and overgrazed. In the foothills, watershed problems caused by land misuse are serious—from Venezuela (where the problem is recognized as acute), through Colombia (where rehabilitation has begun), to Argentina (where clay eroded from the overgrazed watershed of the Bermejo River is carried 1200 kilometers by the Parana River to the sea at Buenos Aires). The 80 million tons of sediment lost each year from the Bermejo watershed requires costly dredging to maintain access to the port.

The Central American Highlands

Upland watersheds in Central America are undergoing extensive deforestation, mainly for cattle raising and agriculture. Land misuse after the loss of forest cover and a general failure to use proper soil conservation techniques are causing widespread soil erosion and land degradation in almost all the watersheds in the region.

The problems are most serious on the steeply sloped Pacific watersheds where most of the population lives and most of the region's food is produced. In many areas, soil erosion has become so severe that the productive potential of the land is being destroyed. Increasing sedimentation threatens present and planned hydropower development throughout the region and is damaging coastal mangrove forests and fisheries.

The Ethiopian Highlands

The Central Highlands Plateau in Ethiopia supports 22 million farmers (70% of the population) and contains 59% of the country's cultivable land. Exhaustive farming practices, overgrazing, and fuelwood collection have severely eroded the plateau and destroyed most forest. Loss of soil fertility is widespread and fertilizer use is so limited that food production has not kept pace with population growth. Drought has precipitated a major famine.

China's Loess Plateau

Enclosed by a bight of the Yellow River in its middle reaches, the Loess Plateau has been subject to soil erosion on a large scale that is unique to China. Erosion has carved the plateau into steep rounded hills and gorges, and roads and bridges have been swept away by torrents and landslides. South of the Great Wall in this region, erosion caused by over-cultivation and neglect of the poverty-stricken rural areas has reduced much fertile land to uninhabited wasteland. China already has nine people per hectare of cropland, and it cannot afford to lose fertile acres on this scale.

Declining Industrial Wood Supplies

Industrial forest products such as sawnwood, plywood, and paper are important throughout the world. They are a source of essential building materials and of the paper needed for schoolbooks, newspapers, and packing. Sustained development of the Third World implies a steady increase in demand for forest products as literacy increases and as the needs for housing, furniture, paper, and other wood-based industries grow.

Developing countries include nearly half the world's closed forests, but they produce only 21% of its industrial timber. Many developing countries have both large natural forests and ecological conditions that are suitable for industrial plantations of fast-growing trees. However, a decline in the area of accessible commercial forests is causing serious problems. In most of these countries forest management and reforestation fall far short of what is needed to limit imports and sustain exports. Exports to industrialized countries are very important for some developing countries, but the most critical problem for the future is the growing inability of many countries to meet their domestic needs for industrial forest products.

Rising imports and declining exports

Imports of forest products by developing countries are increasing sharply, even in such countries as Nigeria, Thailand, and Mexico which should readily be able to supply their own domestic needs. Imports have risen from about US $6 billion in the early 1970s to almost US $10 billion today.

In Mexico for example, the annual value of forest product imports exceeds US $600 million, even though the country has enough forests to be self-sufficient in industrial forest products. Nigeria, once a significant exporter of timber, now imports industrial forest products at a cost of more than US $210 million annually. This nearly equals the value of the 2.5 million tons of food grain currently imported.

Over the past decade, exports of industrial forest products by developing countries have averaged about US $7 billion (1984 prices) and rank fifth overall in non-oil exports. The value of exports has risen sharply during this time, but it is unlikely this rate of growth will continue unless additional investment is made to sustain the productivity of industrial forest resources.

In several countries, notably Cameroon, Gabon, Ivory Coast, Malaysia, and the Philippines, current rates of timber harvesting and insufficient past investment in forest management and reforestation will lead to a sharp decline in exports within 10-15 years. On a smaller scale, the same trend is perceivable in many other countries. In Ghana, for example, exports have fallen from a high of 124 million cubic meters in 1973 to 11 million cubic meters in 1982.

By the end of the century, the 33 developing countries that are now net exporters of forest products will be reduced to less than 10, and total developing country exports of industrial forest products are predicted to drop from their current level of more than US $7 billion to less than US $2 billion.

Many developing countries have both substantial natural forests and ecological conditions suited for fast-growing industrial plantations. Nevertheless, in most such countries forest management and reforestation fall far short of what is needed to limit imports and sustain exports.

Local consumption of forest products has outstripped increases in domestic production and more and more developing countries face burdensome bills for importing forest products. In several countries, exports of forest products have increased, but this growth cannot be sustained without increasing investments to maintain the supply. The most critical countries are:

Africa	Asia	Latin America
Cameroon	Burma	Argentina
Congo	China	Brazil
Gabon	India	Chile
Ghana	Indonesia	Colombia
Ivory Coast	Malaysia	Costa Rica
Liberia	Pakistan	Ecuador
Nigeria	Papua New Guinea	Guatemala
Swaziland	Philippines	Jamaica
Uganda	Thailand	Mexico
Zaire		Peru
		Venezuela

Several factors have contributed to this situation:

- Every year, 5 million hectares of closed tropical forests are logged. Frequently, only a few of the highest valued and more easily marketed species are extracted from uncut forests. This process disturbs much of the remaining vegetation and reduces significantly the commercial value of the secondary forest that grows back.
- When new roads provide access to forests, uncontrolled encroachment by farmers (and in some areas ranchers) often follows. Each year, in ad-

dition to the forests that are logged, more than 7.5 million hectares of closed tropical forests are lost by conversion to agriculture.

■ Reforestation has not kept pace with logging and deforestation. Less than 600,000 hectares of industrial plantations are planted each year in developing countries. This is less than 10% of the area of forest logged or converted.

■ Industrial forest resources have not been well managed. Over the past 30 years, there has been minimal investment in protecting and intensively managing forests already clearcut or selectively logged. Many plantations are not well maintained, protected from fire, or regularly thinned and harvested. Because of poor management, yields from plantation often have been lower than expected.

■ Forest management is also hampered by a shortage of well-trained personnel, insufficient investment in research, and inadequate administrative structures and financing mechanisms.

Threatened Tropical Rain Forests

Tropical rain forests are the most biologically diverse ecosystems on earth. A single hectare of Amazon rain forest can harbor 230 tree species compared with the 10 to 15 species normally found in a hectare of temperate forest. They are estimated to contain almost half of all species of plants and animals. However, most tropical species, especially the insects and other animals, have not yet been described or cataloged by scientists. If destruction of tropical rainforests — which account for 60% of the world's annual loss of forests — continues unabated, an estimated 10-20% of the earth's biological heritage will be gone by the year 2000.

In Madagascar, only 10% of the original forest remains, yet this forest harbors an extraordinarily large number of endemic plants and animals. For example, three families of primates are endemic to the island — more than 20 species are found there and nowhere else. Further loss of Madagascar's remnant patches of tropical forest inevitably will jeopardize many of its endemic species.

Tropical forests yield a wide array of useful products such as essential oils, gums, latexes, resins, tannins, steroids, waxes, edible oils, rattans, bamboo, flavorings, spices, pesticides, and dyestuffs. Many of these materials never enter the commercial market; they are gathered free by local people and are essential to their well-being. But they are also the origin of myriad products manufactured and consumed daily in developed countries, including foods, polishes, insecticides, sedatives, cosmetics, and medicines. In Indonesia alone, rattans (climbing palms used for cane furniture, baskets, and matting) generate substantial export income, and global trade in rattan end-products totals US $4 billion.

More than 50% of modern medicines come from the natural world, many of these from tropical plants. Two anticancer compounds, for example, derive from the periwinkle plant found only in Madagascar. With these anticancer drugs, there is now a 99% chance of remission in children and a 58% chance of remission from Hodgkin's disease. Synthesis of many naturally-derived drugs is not commercially feasible, and even for drugs that can be synthesized, the chemical blueprints provided by wild plants are often needed. In developing countries, where modern medicines are often unavailable or too expensive, naturally derived medicines from undisturbed tropical forests may be the primary source of health care.

The center of origin of many food plants is in the tropics. As tropical lands are converted for human use, ancestral stocks of these plants are jeopardized or lost. Only three species — corn, wheat, and rice — produce two-thirds of the world grain crop. The food supply of the entire world depends on maintaining plant resistance to pests and disease, and resistance is often restored or maintained by cross-breeding with wild populations of the same species. Several wild and domesticated food plant varieties have become extinct and many more are seriously threatened. The gene for semi-dwarfism that improved production in Asian rice came from a primitive Taiwanese cultivar. Resistance to virus probably evolved in the Silent Velley, a seriously threatened region of India. Incorporation of this gene into new rice varieties has greatly benefitted people who depend on this major world crop. Despite these many examples of the usefulness of tropical plants, less than 1% of them have been screened for their potentially useful properties. Agricultural clearing by more than 250 million people who live in tropical forests is increasing. Not only has the population of subsistence farmers grown, but in many nations the absolute amount of cleared land available to them has decreased. The concentration of land-ownership, which has characterized land tenure in the developing world, has become even more pronounced in recent years. Much of this land is used to produce export products, while in many cases per capita food consumption continues to decline.

Expanding agriculture into tropical forests often is futile, however, because the soils are poor or unsuited to continuous production of crops. This is exacerbated by the shortening of the fallow periods because of increasing demands for food. In addition, much good agricultural land now lies fallow, and an even larger amount is managed inefficiently and nonintensively. Improving agricultural efficiency, especially for the small farmer, could greatly reduce pressures on forests.

In Colombia, for example, small farmers produce three times as much food per hectare as do owners of large farms. But because of population increase and land degradation, those same farmers do not now have enough land to pursue their traditional farming lifestyles, and increasingly they move into urban areas or into the forests of Amazonia, where there are now nine times more people than in the mid-1950s.

Cattle ranching has caused widespread loss of tropical forests, especially in Latin America. Overgrazing degrades pasture and limits forest regeneration. Compared with growing crops, raising livestock is a low productivity use of arable land. Much of the meat goes to the cities or is exported to developed countries, with the income primarily benefiting a small number of large land-holders.

Commercial logging affects an estimated 5 million hectares of undisturbed tropical forests each year, and this does not include estimates of illegal logging. Trade records from Thailand and the Philippines, for example, indicate that more trees are logged illegally than legally. Careless logging can lead to ecological damage that is much greater than simply the loss of the logged trees: often 30-60% of residual trees are injured beyond recovery. Large areas are often left bare, leading to soil loss. Logging machinery compacts the soil, reducing water infiltration rates, thereby increasing soil erosion. Most important, logging roads increase access for farmers who clear additional land for agriculture. Such unintentional opening up of forested areas occurs worldwide, and it is particularly serious in Amazonia and southeast Asia.

Building Institutions for Research, Training, and Extension

In many developing countries, two formidable problems in forestry are weak research programs and shortages of trained forestry personnel, including extension workers. Because of inadequate data, weak monitoring capabilities, insufficient operating funds, and the shortage of trained personnel, many forestry administrations simply are unable to implement forestry policies or plan and manage research, training, extension, and other forestry programs.

Recruiting and retaining highly qualified and motivated researchers, teachers, field managers, and extension agents is difficult in tropical countries. Career opportunities are poor, prestige attached to forestry is low, and salaries are inadequate. In all regions, there are shortages of trained forestry staff, particularly at the vocational and technician levels. FAO has estimated that Latin America has the capacity to train a sufficient number of professional foresters but in 1980 the region had a shortage of 12,000 forestry technicians.

Forestry training institutions have been badly neglected in many countries. Curricula for education and training must be revised to reflect the changing needs and priorities in forestry, particularly the emerging emphasis on farm and community forestry. Foresters, traditionally trained to protect government forest reserves and to manage them for industrial wood production, generally lack experience in working with local people and community groups and often are insensitive to their needs. There is an urgent need to increase the amount of practical training, to improve teacher training and training techniques, and to modernize and expand training centers.

Most forestry research institutions, especially those in Africa, are weak. They have shortages of trained researchers, equipment, and operating funds. As with training, forestry research priorities must be made more relevant to the problems facing developing countries today.

Dissemination of forestry information and technologies is poor because of weak links among research, training, and extension and because of poor communication between countries. Few countries have well-developed forestry extension services, and foresters are often drawn to urban areas where career opportunities are greatest.

The Solutions are Known

The prognosis for tropical forests is indeed grim if action is not taken soon. However, there is still a strong basis for hope. Deforestation can be arrested and, ultimately, reversed. Although there have been many failures, decades of experience have demonstrated successful solutions to deforestation and land misuse. However, these efforts have been isolated and on far too small a scale to address the problem effectively.

Based on lessons learned from both successful and unsuccessful experiences in the past, enough is now known to launch a concerted effort on a broad front to combat deforestation. However, the scale of action required cannot possibly be achieved by government foresters alone. An "across-the-board" effort, involving both the public and private sectors, from government ministries to local community groups, is needed in order to rapidly expand tropical forest conservation and development programs.

Governments must take the lead

The long-term success of an expanded program of action will depend on political leadership and appropriate policy changes by developing country governments to support community-level initiatives. Short-term measures will not solve the problem. Neither will narrowly focused action within the forestry sector. A sustained commitment to forestry, agriculture, energy, and related rural development programs is required.

Solutions outside forestry are essential

Because some policies and practices in agriculture, energy, and other sectors lead to forest destruction, many of the solutions to deforestation must come from outside the forestry sector. Priorities include:

- More intensive agriculture and rural development programs to help the 250 million people already living within the tropical moist forests establish sustainable farming systems that do not destroy the forest and to help the millions of people living adjacent to threatened forests to minimize further encroachment.
- Accelerated land reform programs and better employment opportunities that could provide some of the developing world's smallholders and landless people with alternatives to forest clearing or encroachment.
- Greater effort and political commitment to channel future agricultural settlement into nonforest areas and into deforested areas suitable for agriculture.
- Integrated land-use planning that optimizes use of land for agriculture, forestry, conservation, and other productive activities on a sustainable basis, while minimizing the negative impacts of transportation, irrigation, and resettlement schemes on tropical forest ecosystems.
- Research to develop sustainable farming systems that combine trees and food crops on the millions of hectares of marginal lands or wastelands.
- Revision of government fiscal policies outside the forestry sector (such as subsidies for large-scale cattle ranching) that encourage exploitation, depletion, or waste of forest resources to a greater extent than could be economically justified or commercially profitable without government intervention.

The changing role of foresters

To support the changing emphasis in developing countries from industrial to farm and community forestry, foresters and forestry agencies must make some radical changes in their own policies, priorities, and practices. In particular, foresters need to:

- Establish policies that encourage local involvement in forestry activities.
- Work more closely with people at the local level and involve them in identifying, planning, and implementing forest protection and management activities.
- Place more emphasis on mass-media publicity and extension support for forestry conservation and development on farmlands and wastelands

outside government-controlled forest reserves. Through education and extension programs, encourage recognition of trees and forests as worthwhile "crops" to be cared for in their own right.

- Decentralize tree seedling production and other forestry operations and involve individuals more directly in these activities through local community groups, nongovernmental organizations, and schools.
- Give more attention to conservation programs that can help to increase protection of and research on tropical rain forests.
- Use lower cost technologies such as direct seeding and more intensive mass-production techniques to accelerate tree planting programs.
- Place greater emphasis on multipurpose trees to provide people with timber, poles, fuelwood, fruit, fodder, fiber, and other nonwood forest products.
- Intensify research on agroforestry and management of secondary or degraded forests.
- Modify and expand forestry training and education programs to place greater emphasis on extension skills, agroforestry, and conservation of forest ecosystems.
- Refrain from converting natural forests to plantations when other suitable land is available.
- Revise government fiscal policies in forestry, such as lenient forest concession agreements, to encourage sustainable management of natural forests and plantations.
- Quantify more precisely the negative effect of deforestation on agricultural productivity, employment, rural incomes, and the balance of trade.
- Work more closely with planners in agriculture, energy, industry, and other sectors to design broadly based agriculture and energy programs in which forestry will play a vital, though not always the lead, role.

Local participation determines success

As important as political leadership is to the success of an expanded program of action, the key ingredient is active participation by the millions of small farmers and landless people who daily use forests and trees to meet their needs. Countless rural development projects have failed to make a long-term impact because of inadequate involvement of local people. Greater attention must be given to creating incentives for local participation and ensuring that communities are involved meaningfully in project planning and implementation. The roles of women and nongovernmental organizations merit special attention.

Creating incentives

Governments need to establish policies that encourage local participation in rural tree planting programs and natural forest management. Forestry codes and laws affecting land and tree tenure; prices for poles, fuelwood, fruit, and other forest products; and the cost and availability of seeds and seedlings of desired species need to be reassessed as potential incentives or disincentives to participation.

Incentives must also be incorporated into development project design. People will not participate in tree planting or related activities if they do not perceive it to be in their interest. Project design must be based on sufficient knowledge of local social, cultural, and ecological conditions as well as of people's perceptions and attitudes. Local participants in a project must be assured of reaping the benefits of their labor.

Involving women

Women play important and in many regions dominant roles in agricultural and livestock production and in the use and management of trees. An increasingly apparent trend in rural areas is the rise in the number of woman-headed households. As a result, women are assuming new roles and responsibilities.

Women and children often suffer disproportionately from deforestation and its aftermath. Women generally are responsible for collecting fuelwood. As fuelwood becomes scarce, they must spend more and more time gathering it and are thus diverted from other household, childcare, or revenue-earning tasks.

Despite the important economic and social roles of women, forestry and other rural development projects continue to be designed without adequately considering their effect on women or the role of women in their implementation. Although their role in development projects is often overlooked, women have made important contributions. For example, they have carried out soil conservation measures (Lesotho), planted trees (China, El Salvador, Honduras), done nursery work (India), introduced and promoted the use of fuel-efficient stoves (Honduras), and led conservation movements (Chipko movement in India).

More and better information on women's work patterns, their role in the community, and their perceptions of problems and solutions is needed. This requires more involvement of women in extension work. Women must also be adequately represented at the professional level in program planning and project design.

Nongovernmental organizations: a bridge to the local level

Special attention needs to be paid to the role of nongovernmental organizations (NGOs) in managing and maintaining natural tropical forests and in tree planting. An estimated 5,000 NGOs are involved in forestry worldwide, and hundreds of organizations aim, as their primary purpose, to protect forests or to rehabilitate degraded areas.

NGOs, working effectively at the local level, often over a long period and with small amounts of money, can do much to stimulate community involvement in forestry. NGOs often can act as intermediaries between government bureaucracies and local people, and many projects are carried out by NGOs, often with major funding from the development assistance agencies. The role of NGOs in forestry is expanding rapidly, and their involvement will be a vital ingredient in overcoming forestry problems in most developing countries.

Development assistance agencies can do more

Development assistance allocations to forestry are small, particularly in relation to the magnitude of the problems. Worse, they are declining relative to other sectors. The World Bank and the Inter-American, Asian and African Development Banks allocate approximately 1% of their annual financing to forestry, the U.N. Development Program (UNDP) only 2%. The allocation is increasing, but it remains a very small portion of total development assistance.

Forestry's crucial role in sustaining agricultural productivity and its other contributions to economic development is unrecognized because forestry activities do not always bring short-term political or economic gains. Short-term efforts to expand agricultural production usually takes precedence over forest conservation and environmental protection programs.

Experience in rural development has shown that how money is spent is even more important than how much. The greater emphasis on farm and community forestry and watershed management requires new approaches to project planning and operations. These projects, which involve changing people's land-use practices, require local participation in their design and implementation. This has important implications for the development assistance agencies and their *modus operandi*.

Greater attention must be given to human and social factors. Information on local social and cultural conditions should be systematically collected and incorporated into development project design. Project planning and implementation should be more flexible and emphasize a "bottom-up" approach. Decision-making should be decentralized as much as possible. Strengthening the capabilities of national forestry and related institutions, particularly in working at the local level, must be a major investment priority.

Often, small amounts of funding are needed over long periods for this type of activity.

Better coordination among development assistance agencies and within single agencies is needed to avoid duplication of effort, working at cross-purposes, or burdening developing country agencies with funding and administrative demands that exceed their absorptive capacity. For example, mechanisms are needed to ensure that agricultural intensification efforts (livestock and cropping) consider and accommodate local needs for fuel-wood and other forest products. Similarly, infrastructure development (e.g., transportation and irrigation schemes) and resettlement schemes must be planned and coordinated to avoid wasting or destroying forest resources, jeopardizing forest conservation areas, or making easily accessible forest areas that are unsuited for agriculture in the long term.

The most successful forestry development projects have been those where a combination of national government effort, political commitment, and external aid, has triggered a spontaneous response from local farmers, communities, and the private sector for large-scale self-sustaining programs.

An Agenda for Action: Planning a Five-year Program

In developing the action plan to address deforestation issues on a broad front, the Task Force used the following guidelines:

- High priority countries were identified based on previous studies by the U.N. Food and Agriculture Organization, leading multilateral and bilateral aid agencies, and such nongovernmental organizations as the International Union for Conservation of Nature and Natural Resources.
- Priorities for action were to accord closely with those identified as important by national governments and leading multilateral and bilateral aid agencies. Accordingly, the five priority areas for action identified in FAO's Tropical Forest Action Program and endorsed by the FAO Committee on Forest Development in the Tropics were adopted.
- The proposals were to be based on successful and well-documented development projects and were to consider lessons learned from development project failures.
- Special attention was paid to identifying small-scale projects that have potential for widespread replicability.
- Past projects were examined in terms of their success in involving local people. Special emphasis was given to projects with high economic rates of return that have the potential to be self-sustaining.

■ Investment needs were treated in the broadest sense to include support for institution-strengthening activities, including research, training, and extension which experience has shown account for 15-25% of total investment requirements.

■ Besides examining priorities in forestry, investment needs were estimated for related agricultural activities, and agricultural development was considered to be an integral part of any program of accelerated investment.

■ Special account was taken of a country's capacity to absorb new investment. This is an important factor in limiting investment in the short term.

The Task Force estimated the level of public and private investent needed to make an impact on tropical deforestation over the next 5 years to be US $8 billion. About US $5.3 billion (two-thirds of the total) would be needed for the 56 most seriously affected countries reviewed in its report.

At least 30% of the proposed investment would be related to agriculture. The primary objective would be to provide farmers and landless people living in or adjacent to threatened tropical forests, in overpopulated uplands, and semiarid areas with an alternative to destroying forests and woodlands.

Half of the total US $8 billion, or US $800 million each year for 5 years, would need to be mobilized by the development assistance agencies and international lending institutions such as The World Bank. The remainder would come directly from national governments and the private sector. Investment of US $800 million a year in forestry and related agricultural development would about double the present levels of external aid in these areas.

Conclusion

Despite the grim prognosis for tropical forests, the basis for hope is strong. Deforestation can be arrested and, ultimately, reversed. Decades of experience have demonstrated many successful solutions to deforestation and related land misuse. However, these efforts too often have been isolated and far too small to address the problem effectively. We need now increased political awareness of deforestation's negative impacts on human welfare and the environment and the political will to mobilize the human and financial resources to do something about it.

Will it happen? There are very encouraging signs that the development assistance community now recognizes the repercussions of deforestation that reach far beyond the forestry sector alone, and that development projects in other sectors such as agriculture depend on maintaining forests, soils, and upland watersheds. Also, the international nongovernmental organizations are publicizing the loss of forests and helping to build the grassroots constituency needed to force political action. It remains to be seen, however, whether some of the developing country governments will commit themselves to conserving their forests. The debt burden facing many of these countries makes them hesitate to seek additional loans from the multilateral banks, and aid in the form of grants from developed country agencies will be insufficient by itself. Since the fall of 1985 when the Action Plan was released, FAO and the development agencies have made considerable progress in implementing parts of the Plan. An Action Plan Secretariat has been established at FAO headquarters in Rome, and it is coordinating forestry sector reviews in more than 20 countries. Twelve countries are in the process of developing national tropical forestry action plans. The World Bank has substantially revised and expanded its lending program for Africa, and three countries (The Netherlands, France, and Germany) have committed to doubling their development assistance in forestry in the next two years. Nongovernmental organizations have not been actively involved in forestry in most countries, but in more than 20 tropical countries they are beginning to participate directly in developing national forestry plans. The big question is whether all these actions are enough — and soon enough.

Finally, one irony of the deforestation crisis is that the level of funding needed to halt widespread forest destruction is minuscule when compared to the annual private philanthropy or defense expenditures by the industrialized nations of the world.

References

1. Asian Development Bank, 1980, "Sector Paper on Forestry and Forest Industry," Asian Development Bank, Manila, Philippines.

2. Erwin, T.L., 1982, "Tropical forests: their richness in coleoptera and other arthropod species," Coleopterists Bulletin, 36:74-75.

3. FAO/UNEP, 1981, "Tropical Forests Resources Assessment Project: Tropical Africa, Tropical Asia, Tropical America," FAO, Rome.

4. FAO, 1985, "Tropical Forestry Action Plan," FAO, Rome. 5. Furtado, Jose I., 1986, "The future of tropical forests," pp.145-171, *in*, Nicholas Polunin, editor, "Ecosystem Theory and Application," John Wiley and Sons, Ltd., London.

6. Myers, N., 1980, "Conversion of Tropical Moist Forests," National Academy of Sciences, Washington, D.C.

7. OTA, 1984, "Technologies to Sustain Tropical Forest Resources," U.S. Congress, Office of Technology Assessment, Washington, D.C.

8. Prance, G.T., and T.S. Elias, editors, 1977, "Extinction is Forever," New York Botanical Garden, Bronx, New York.

9. Raven, P.H., 1980, "Research Priorities in Tropical Biology," National Research Council, Washington, D.C.

10. Sommer, A., 1976, "An attempt at an assessment of the world's tropical moist forests," Unasylva 28(112-113):5-24.

11. Whitmore, T.C., 1984, "Tropical rain forests of the Far East," second edition, revised, Clarendon Press, Oxford.

12. World Bank, 1978, "Forestry, A Sector Policy Paper," The World Bank, Washington, D.C.

13. World Resources Institute, The World Bank, and the United Nations Development Program, 1985, "Tropical Forests: A Call For Action," World Resources Institute, Washington, D.C.

14. World Resources Institute and the International Institute for Environment and Development, 1986, "World Resources 1986," Basic Books, New York.

Comments on <u>Tropical Forests: A Resource in Jeopardy</u>

Prof. Dr. E. El-Hinnawi
National Research Centre,
Cairo, Egypt

This paper should be thoroughly revised to justify several statements and more important to reference quantitative information and important statements. References are totally lacking.

The paper draws on several published reports: Reports by the United Nations Environment Program, World Watch Institute and documents of the United Nations Conference on New and Renewable Sources of Energy.

Some of the data need updating. For example, the rate of deforestation on p. 3 should be 11.3 million ha/y according to recent UNEP/FAO assessments. On p. 6, reference to amount of dung burned annually should be given. This value is underestimated. The data related to fuelwood on p. 8 are essentially those in the document on fuelwood presented at the UN Conference on New and Renewable sources of Energy. These should be updated.

The paper repeats what has been said about tropical forests and deforestation over the last five years or so. I would have liked to see a more in-depth assessment of the socio-economic and environmental aspects of destruction of tropical forests, and also of afforestation programs in some countries. Several existing reports outline recommendations like the ones presented in this paper. But what has happened, say in the last 5 years? Are afforestation efforts in Indonesia, Thailand, the Philippines, Kenya, etc. successful? If so, why and what are the impacts of such undertakings. If not, why and what are the constraints. IFIAS should focus on such issues.

Members of the staff of El Colegio de Mexico

This paper is not clear as to the causes of worldwide deforestation. It omits other factors than the ones mentioned, particularly in relation to tropical forests. This term is used imprecisely in the paper, sometimes referring to forests in nontropical areas (e.g. Chile).

As to the responsibility of the rural population, what is said on page 1 contradicts what is stated on page 3, para. 5. The responsibility of the rural poor is perhaps exaggerated.

In Latin America, deforestation in tropical areas can be ascribed to: pressure from stockraising interests in favor of extensive exploitation; the interests of holders of forestry concessions; the depredation carried out by large multinationals (e.g. in Brazil); large projects supported by multilateral agencies (e.g. the IDB backing to the Chontalpa development in southeast Mexico, the World Bank support for land clearing in Central America for meat production).

The paper also exaggerates the impact of population pressure on resources; for instance, in some cases, population density increases *as a result of* large forestry exploitation. To say that demographic density largely explains the difference between the treatment of forests in developed countries and developing countries seems a gross simplification; the climatic factors should be taken into account. The ecological richness of tropical jungle is not mentioned. Some sparsely-populated areas (e.g. Chile) have witnessed destruction of forests. In general, the paper fails to indicate what can be done to rationally use the tropical forests.

Don Scott-Kemmis
Centre for Technology & Social Change
The University of Wollongong, Australia

This paper reflects a process of reassessment which began to gather pace about a decade ago, and which has since developed with increasing urgency. The FAO *Tropical Forest Action Plan* (1985) (hereafter referred to as TFAP) and the complementary reports of a 'task force' convened by the World Resources Institute, The World Bank and UNDP, are the product of sustained efforts to assess, draw attention to, and find paths out of, a growing crisis of immense proportions. This paper outlines the main thrust of these reports. The priorities in the current phase of activity are twofold:

■ To generate increased commitment and financial flows from multi-lateral and bilateral agencies; and to develop both political awareness and detailed action plans at the national level within developing countries.

The statistics enumerated in this paper — the many millions of people and very extensive land areas directly threatened by resource degradation — convey some aspects of the magnitude of the situation. The paper also emphasizes the powerful and self-reinforcing negative dynamic which underlines the many-faceted problem — the trinity of 'poverty, skewed land distribution and low agricultural productivity.'

Burley and Hazlewood's excellent overview identifies the major types of forest-land degradation and the ecological, social and economic processes that underly them. They focus attention on those types of effort and directions of change which appear to offer the greatest potential for reversing this degradation. The international and national programs that are now being developed deserve substantial support.

The obstacles which must be faced in designing and implementing effective action should be recognized clearly at the outset. For understandable reasons the recent reports and plans which seek to stimulate change and activity do not dwell on these. The following comments focus on two key obstacles — one a very broad issue and the second more specific.

First, the 'roots of the problem' as diagnosed by Burley and Hazlewood (and the TFAP) are very deep indeed. Marginal shifts in resource allocation at international or national levels can do a great deal to stimulate change but are most unlikely to redirect to the extent required the powerful dynamics. Burley and Hazlewood emphasize both the need for political commitment at the national level, and for a major reorientation of rural development policy. But they do not draw out the implications of these priorities. Implicit in their paper is the expectation that action programs of various types will stimulate a *process* of change which will grow and deepen over time. They suggest that there is an enormous latent potential for major change which can be given momentum and direction through well-designed interventions. for example, they place considerable emphasis on the role of 'grassroots' responses by NGO's and informal village level organizations and on essentially 'private' investment (at community or farm levels) in tree planting.

The fate of forests and woodlands is clearly tied to the fate of the poorer rural groups, whose fate in turn depends on the success of a vigorous and broadly based rural development. Some evidence does encourage optimism about the latent potential for major change. But if that process of change is to be effective then forestry-related activities must act as the 'cutting edge' for deep and sustained innovation in rural society, institutions and development approaches. The international community in general, and those concerned with rural development in particular have an important role in ensuring that, insofar as possible, forestry-related reappraisals and activities effect such a far-reaching process of change. For well known reasons the UN agencies and the bilateral agencies are constrained in the extent to which they can actively play such an unavoidable political role. Nevertheless it is essential that the scope for influence be explored and exploited. One less problematical means of contributing to this objective would be to strengthen developing country capacities for monitoring and for policy research and analysis.

The second issue on which these comments focus concerns the strengthening of capacities, at all levels within developing countries, for vigorous technical change. The generation and diffusion of improved technologies have an essential role in effective responses to forest-land degradation. Burley and Hazlewood (along with the TFAP) emphasize the importance of *diffusing* existing organizational and technical knowledge – i.e., to get on with applying 'available' knowledge rather than delay action until further research generates new knowledge. They do however draw attention to the necessity for building or greatly improving research, training and extension institutions in order to develop a local knowledge acquisition, generation and delivery system which is effective in responding to local needs.

Programs to strengthen these capacities will be a critical element for successful and sustained action, yet the path forward is far from clear. Weaknesses in forestry research and extension institutions like similar weaknesses in comparable agricultural institutions arise in part from under-investment, institutional isolation and rigidities in organization and approach. Overcoming these weaknesses is a major challenge because:

- the necessity to rapidly expand the rate of investment and of technical improvements in forestry-related activities will require considerable capacities to acquire, modify, diffuse and further improve a diverse range of technologies;
- forestry-related institutions and policies are undergoing a process of radical reorientation to address new objectives and target groups, and involving the evolution of new inter-institutional linkages;
- the process of institutional change and strengthening will involve considerable time and innovative effort.

But designing and implementing change along these lines is an enormous challenge – the success of past efforts has been very uneven, there is a paucity of relevant prior experience, and effective approaches will have to evolve for specific local contexts. While there is a growing consensus around the broad objectives which might guide this process there is far less agreement (and knowledge) about the means by which such goals can be translated into specific programs, and human resources requirements. Here again, the international community can contribute substantially by assisting the collection, analysis and dissemination of relevant experience as well as by direct efforts to strengthen key scientific, technical and managerial capacities in developing countries.

In short, the growing catastrophe cannot be averted through a 'green tree revolution' – although something of that sort must occur. It is essential to assist developing countries to build those types of dynamic capacity which can identify and effectively respond to local problems.

Dr. Pamela Stokes
Institute for Environmental Studies, Canada

The text reads well; the paper is very informative, and the opinions quite sane and reasonable. It smacks a little of 'motherhood'.

The main question in my mind was with respect to potential readership. In places it reads like a graduate review paper.

My main criticism concerns the complete lack of citations or evidence to back up the statements which are made. There are notes to this effect, in pencil throughout the text.

I wish to put on record that I asked a colleague, Professor Spencer Barrett, who has worked in and lectured on tropical forests, to read this paper and he concurred with my opinions.

Apart from any other considerations, the interested reader may want to follow up some of the information, so at the very least, a bibliography is required. On a more technical level, statements involving numbers, statistics etc., are not very strong unless supported by documentation, source or reference. The paper will be much more useful and much more convincing if the proposed information is included.

2

Dimensions of a New Vulnerability: The Significance of Large-scale Urbanization in Developing Countries

Ian Burton
IFIAS, Toronto, Canada

Some Basic Facts

A dramatic transformation is taking place in the form and distribution of human settlements. In those regions of the world where the total population is growing most rapidly, cities are growing much more rapidly. In short, the developing world is becoming a world of cities. The Third World has been thought of as a region of raw materials and agricultural production, supplying natural resource inputs to the urban-industrial complexes of the metropolitan nations in "the North." This image must now be changed to one in which teeming cities have a dominant place. Urbanization in the Third World is not entirely a new phenomenon (Davis 1969), but the pace of change and the sheer size of the new mega-cities being created are new. According to U.N. estimates, about 25% of the population of the less developed regions of the world lived in cities in 1975. By the year 2000, it will reach about 40%. In absolute numbers, the urban population of the less developed regions is expected to increase from 775 million to 1,996 million in 25 years, much of the growth taking place in cities of one million people and more. Estimates are shown in Table 1.

Consider for a moment how this translates into the task of city building. In 25 years, the world's stock of housing, transport facilities, water supply and sanitation systems, factories, offices and commercial establishments will

Table 1. Urban and rural populations in presently more and less developed regions

Quantity	Presently more developed regions		Presently less developed regions	
	1975	2000	1975	2000
Population size (millions)				
Urban population of which:	783	1107	775	1996
Million-cities	262	447	244	916
Other urban population	521	660	531	1080
Rural population	349	254	2060	2896
Total population	1132	1361	2835	4892
Average growth rates (per cent per year), 1975-2000				
Urban population of which:	1.4		3.8	
Million-cities	2.1		5.4	
Other urban population	1.0		2.9	
Rural population	-1.3		1.4	
Total population	1.0		2.2	
Percentage relationships				
Urban in total population	69.2	81.4	27.3	40.8
Million-cities in:				
Urban population	33.5	40.4	31.4	45.9
Total population	23.2	32.9	8.6	18.7

Source: Global Review of Human Settlements: Statistical Annex (A/CONF.70/A/1Add.1), tables 1, 5, and 6.

have to be more than doubled. The same applies to employment, productive capacity, education, and health services. While doubling is taking place, much of the existing stock must be replaced because it is outworn and inadequate to serve the needs of those who now depend on it. It is a herculean task by any standards. If it can be achieved, there will still be much more to do after the year 2000. The 40% urban population of the Third World may eventually grow to 80%. An urbanization strategy to accommodate so many people in cities will require policies, management, technology and investment well beyond anything yet seen or perhaps even contemplated.

Are Cities Necessary?

Considering the magnitude of this task, it is being asked more frequently if such large-scale urbanization is necessary. The organization of the international economy has largely been managed through cities and the communications and control structures that they wield and serve as nodes. To the extent therefore that developing countries plan to develop by playing a growing role in the international economy and the world division of labor, then some urbanization is necessary.

Cities, especially primate cities, are growing larger and more rapidly than required by need to participate effectively in the world economy. Short of impracticable and unacceptably draconian methods, cities will go on growing well into the next century and many "millionaire" cities are likely to appear as well as a few gargantuan metropolitan centers of 10 to 20 million and more.

That such large-scale urbanization is not likely to be needed in the future is suggested by the so-called U-turn phenomenon in the United States (and perhaps elsewhere in Europe and Japan) whereby the movement of population to the major cities has now ceased and is being reversed.

People are migrating away from the very large cities and are exhibiting a distinct preference for life in smaller cities and towns. Modern electronic and communications technology now makes access to many of the "high-order" metropolitan services as easy if not easier in smaller communities. The wave of the future may well be, therefore, a dispersal of economic activity and population away from larger cities in the developed world towards smaller towns.

As in other development processes, it is always tempting to think that developing countries might leap-frog the stages and move towards a more regionally balanced urbanization without the necessity of going though the phase of excessive urbanization of a few major centers. While such a desirable eventuality might find acceptance as a policy goal, its achievement in the short or medium-term (20-25 years) is most improbable. The social and demographic forces at work will largely work themselves out in their own good time. Efforts by government at major deflections of this course are not likely to achieve anything more than "fine tuning." Cities are certainly needed. Such large cities are not, but we will, in all likelihood, get them anyway.

Comparative Urbanization

Third World urbanization, now proceeding in top gear, is not a simple repetition in the tropical world of events that took place in temperate latitudes at an earlier date. While there are important similarities, these are not sufficient to provide reassurance that the modern cities of "the north" are in the process of being recreated in "the south."

The differences are profound (Berry, 1981). We are essentially dealing with a new phenomenon never before seen on the face of the planet. It is incumbent upon us in those circumstances to bring a fresh eye to the urbanization of the Third World unclouded by preconceived notions of what is urbanization and where it might lead.

In the 19th century industrial urbanization, many men were drawn to the cities by the prospect of factory employment. Women came for marriage rather than paid employment (Weber, 1899). The housing and sanitary conditions were as shocking to contemporary observers like Charles Dickens as they are today in the Third World cities. At the beginning of the century, deaths exceeded births in the cities, which would have actually declined the population, had it not been for the large-scale migration from agricultural areas to small towns, and thence into the major centers. It was not until near the end of the century that the high urban death rate had been brought down and cities were beginning to produce a surplus of births (Weber, 1899).

In many parts of the Third World today, 20-50% of the population growth of cities results from natural increase. Migrants come in search of employment but do not always find it. The 19th century European migrant came to the city with high prospects of employment but at considerable health risk. Today the level of health achieved in many Third World cities is higher than in the rural areas and higher than in the 19th century Europe, but the risk of long-term unemployment is considerable.

Rapid urbanization is taking place in countries with some of the lowest levels of development, where life expectancy at birth, nutrition levels, energy consumption per capita, and education levels are all among the lowest in the world. Such conditions were not much better in 19th century European and North American urbanization, but those nations were leading the economic expansion of world trade and industry, and the economic and social change occurred comparatively gradually over most of the century. The

Third World countries of today are following in the path of development, not leading it, and, starting at a similar level, have achieved similar gains in death-control in 20 to 30 years in stead of 80 to 100.

In the countries of "the north," urbanization was a comparatively slower process that involved what can now be seen as incremental economic development and social change, interacting with each other.

Industrial development was promoted by craftsmen and small entrepreneurs more in advance of urbanization or contemporaneously with it. In the Third World today, social changes are being achieved rapidly through government intervention on a scale unheard of in 19th century Europe and North America. University-educated bureaucrats have been more successful in promoting public welfare, international aid, subsidized housing, free universal education and basic health care than they have been in promoting industrial entrepreneurship and employment and wealth-creating economic growth. Industrialization lags far behind urbanization in the Third World today and attempts to correct the evils of urban poverty by social measures are often serving to make conditions worse by attracting yet more migrants and encouraging more natural increase without commensurate economic growth.

Despite superficial similarities, contemporary urbanization in the Third World is fundamentally different from urbanization in the west. But a theoretical understanding of this new urbanization phenomenon has not yet been developed, and lacking proper understanding, the prescriptions being written still tend to follow in a rather slavish manner the experience of other cities in other places at another time.

The Third World City Characterized

It is misleading to think of Third World urbanization as a distinctly different but essentially uniform phenomenon. There are great differences between the urbanization process in Latin America, Africa and Asia. And within those convenient regional groupings, there is great national diversity. For this reason, caution is necessary in attempting generalizations. No one analysis can suit all circumstances and urban policies and management strategies need to be tailored to the individual conditions of nation states.

Nevertheless, it is useful to consider some of the characteristics which, in varying degrees, many Third World cities have in common. Foremost, among these is very rapid growth of population in excess of employment opportunities. The consequences are that large proportions of the population are poor and cannot therefore provide adequately for themselves. And because economic growth is lagging, governments at local and national levels have woefully inadequate financial resources to apply to the problems created.

Heavy income tax on the emerging middle class and heavy taxes on industry and trade have a potentially negative and crippling effect on economic growth and, in any case, do not yield nearly enough revenue. Taxes on middle income groups and on the entrepreneurially successful, whether indigenous or foreign, tend to discourage capital savings and investment and promoting flight rather than providing a source of attraction.

That people continue to flock to the cities, especially the very largest ones, is testimony to the character of urban and rural life. The poor quality of rural existence is a major "push" factor. Chronic overpopulation in the rural areas means that the growing number of landless rural farm population find it increasingly hard to subsist.

City and national governments try to respond to the urban expansion by providing necessary housing, transport, water supply, sanitation, facilities and health, education and welfare services. Poor as these are, they are better than nonexistent services in the countryside, and in time, tend to attract even more people.

One wage earner in the "formal" economy of private corporations or government organizations commonly supports an extended family of 8 to 10 people. The majority of the work force cannot find a niche in the formal employment economy. The more fortunate engage in a legitimate bazaar-trade often run as a family business. For the rest, there is the increasingly "informal economy," moving from quasi-legitimate street trade of hawkers and vendors, to increasingly marginal and illegitimate activities, including begging, sifting through refuse for reusable or saleable items, theft, petty crime and prostitution. Between 25 and 40% of the urban "work force" may be engaged in this "street-economy" sector. Such persons earn enough money for bare subsistence at best, and often share any windfall surplus with their kin. Intense competition for any income-generating niche keeps earnings at the subsistence minimum and steps to expand employment by investment in directly productive activities, infrastructure or services are soon offset by more migrants.

Squatter, Peripheral and Transitional Settlements

Governments are naturally apprehensive about the growth of a huge new urban class of poor people. This class is not strictly the urban proletariat of Marxist literature for it is not composed of "workers" in the industrial or factory sense. It tends to be composed of migrant families, extended rather than nuclear, living in slum settlements, or more often in unauthorized squatter settlements. Housing is of poor quality often consisting of scavenged materials; water supply of doubtful quality and unreliable quantity is obtained from public standpipes at a distance, from water vendors or even from hand-dug shallow wells and surface streams. Unemployment is high, and much of the income is obtained from the informal "street-economy." Nutrition standards are poor, health standards low, transport facilities overburdened, pests, rodents and insect disease vectors abound, education is not always available, and often not extending beyond primary level in any case.

Despite seemingly overwhelming adversity, the new class in squatter settlements demonstrates remarkable resourcefulness and ingenuity in improving their own conditions. Often unrecognized by governments, such communities frequently have well organized social structures and support networks. Links to the rural areas from which they come are well maintained, and often there is periodic movement back and forth between city and country according to variations in demands for agricultural labor.

There are two quite divergent understandings of the squatter settlements. Governments and many "official" views tend to see them as unwholesome, unclean blots on landscape, symptoms of decay and a threat to orderly progress of development.

A contrary view is that they are in fact a solution rather than a problem. They provide housing on a do-it-yourself basis that the formally constituted authorities cannot produce. The cohesive society continues to provide its own basic requirements and provides its own social security system. As a reception area for newcomers to the city, the squatter settlements assist in the adaptation to urban life of former rural populations. While formal employment is not available, ingenuity is used to obtain a subsistence level income. The settlements often cluster close to those sources of income, thus demands on the formal sector are reasonable low. The squatter settlements assist in the encouragement of small-scale entrepreneurship. It is in these peripheral, transitional settlements that the new city of the Third World is being created.

Official policy in many countries is still to discourage or ignore this crucible of the new urbanization. They are sometimes torn down, bulldozed flat or deliberately burnt while their inhabitants are placed in buses or lorries and sent "back to the villages." While such extreme measures are uncommon, a policy of ignoring the squatter settlements and refusing to deal with them or provide services for fear of legitimizing them, is much more common.

Only haltingly and cautiously are a few Third World governments, and their international helpers, coming to the view that in such people and in such communities may lie the future hope for successful urban development.

The Vulnerability and Resilience of Cities

There is some truth in both polar views of urbanization by squatter settlements in the Third World cities today. They represent a condition of extreme and growing vulnerability that is a true case for concern. At the same time, they contain important elements of resilience that can be focussed and strengthened.

"Vulnerability" and "resilience" are useful concepts to apply to human use systems including systems of settlements, but it should not be supposed that greater precision or scientific credibility will thereby automatically be conferred on the user. The concepts are useful but slithery. On the one hand, they encourage the probing questioning of present trends in urbanization — is greater vulnerability being created and, if so, how? What constitutes urban resilience in the Third World cities of today and how can it be strengthened?

On the other hand, it is not possible to arrive at a precise and stable definition of vulnerability that will be operational and permit qualitative measurement. Measures that reduce vulnerability for individuals, households or communities may increase it for societies and nations, and vice-versa. Even the direction of desired change may therefore be in doubt. Plans to expand electricity generation with the use of nuclear generating stations may simultaneously reduce vulnerability to dramatic changes in the market supply of energy (an oil crisis) while at the same time exposing the population to more low level radiation and some risk of major accidents. The choice of policy or action which produces a minimal "net vulnerability" presents severe difficulties of analysis and judgement. The difficulties are compounded where great divergencies are found between scientific/technical perceptions of vulnerability and those of lay or non-technical persons who perceive themselves to be at risk.

For the present purposes, vulnerability and resilience may be defined as:

Vulnerability: the degree to which a system (or part of a system) may be adversely effected by an event or perturbation usually from "external" sources.

Resilience: the capacity of a system (or part of a system) to absorb and recover from a damaging event or perturbation. The state to which a system recovers is an important theoretical point. Since all systems are in course of change, it is usually inappropriate to think of recovery to the pre-existing conditions. Nevertheless, this mode of thinking often dominates social response to adverse events. The social shock registered by an earthquake or a flood seems to arouse a passion for fighting back and recreating the previous conditions. Such attempts to return to an original condition may serve to enhance subsequent vulnerability rather than reduce it. The more effective forms of resilience (one may say true resilience) seeks to understand the evolutionary trend and adapt to it. Indeed, times of disaster or adverse events (perturbations) often provide excellent opportunities to make adaptive changes that would otherwise be impossible. After the Second World War, a few cities were rebuilt on entirely new lines (Coventry, Rotterdam). Most were reconstructed closely along existing lines. Similarly, after a major earthquake, cities may be simply reconstructed as before or the opportunity may be taken (rarely in practice) to reconstruct the city in such a manner as to make it less vulnerable to future earthquakes. There is an analogous case to be made in relation to trends as opposed to events. In addition to the growth of the vulnerability to events, the Third World cities today are becoming more vulnerable because of the way authorities attempt to cope with adverse and worsening conditions. Just as the city rebuilders after a war or an earthquake have the previously existing city in mind, so do the planners and authorities in Third World cities today have the European and North American cities of the 19th (or even 20th) century in mind. The model is poorly chosen. What is needed is original, fresh thinking about the conditions required to create the less vulnerable and more resilient city.

Before this can be attempted, we must consider the kinds of vulnerability which are growing in Third World cities today.

Types of Vulnerability

All parts of an urban system may be vulnerable so the manner of identifying types of vulnerability depends on the way we choose to disaggregate "the urban system." For present purposes five areas of vulnerability are considered important. These may be labelled as:

   (i) biological (health)
   (ii) structural (the built environment)
   (iii) life support (supplies)
   (iv) economic (income)
   (v) functional (organizations)

(i) Biological vulnerability refers to the susceptibility of human population to disease, injury and death. Thus the impact of any event or any trend may be measured in terms of the extent to which the health of the population is adversely affected in the number of cases of disease, injury or death.

Clearly, some major gains have been made in the health conditions in the cities in developing countries. We have already seen how the level of health is better than in the 19th century European cities. Nevertheless, there are important new elements.

The rapid growth of squatter settlements without adequate water supply, sewerage or solid waste disposal systems and the presence of disease vectors (insects, rodents), added to the poor quality of construction, means that a condition of extreme vulnerability to disease exists. That the mortality rate among children is not much higher is remarkable, and the conditions for rapid deterioration are present in systems so close to the brink. The struggle to maintain a grip on the existing disease risks already exceeds the capacity of responsible authorities. If a new disease should emerge, an event not unknown in human history, (Zinsser, 1935, McNeill, 1976), then the catastrophe could exceed the effects of the plague in 14th century Europe.

To the catalogue of well-known disease risks must also be added the dangers to life and health of modern technology. The recent tragedy at Bhopal in India dramatizes the situation. Over 2000 people were killed and many more permanently handicapped by the accidental release of toxic gas from a pesticide plant. Whatever the causes of the event, there can be no doubt that the consequences were greatly increased by the high concentration of squatter housing in the immediate vicinity of the plant.

This highlights a general problem with squatter settlements. Because they are unplanned, and frequently illegal, they tend to be in marginal or dangerous locations. They are therefore exposed not only to hazards from industrial establishments, but also natural hazards such as flood and landslides.

There is also the danger to health from chronic exposure to the new chemicals. Pesticides alone are estimated to poison as many as 500,000 people, actually killing an estimated 10,000 people in developing countries every year (Mpinga, 1985). This threat may be more evident in rural areas than in the cities, but the general chemicalization of the environment, including food chains, is a problem that taxes the scientific management skills of industrial societies with abundant scientific manpower (Whyte and Burton, 1980). The monitoring of toxic chemicals in developing countries has scarcely begun.

(ii) Structural vulnerability refers to the possibility of loss or damage to the physical existence of the city or the stock of real property. Poor quality of construction in squatter settlements and elsewhere accounts in part for the high loss of life, often suffered in extreme natural events (earthquakes, floods, hurricanes, typhoons and tidal waves). Vulnerability to fire is also high due to several factors—the close proximity of housing often built with highly combustible materials, coupled with difficulty of access for fire-fighting equipment, and critical lack of water supply or water pressure.

(iii) Life-support vulnerability refers to the possibility of the absence, scarcity or disruption in supply of essential supports for life such as water, food, and (depending upon climatic conditions) clothing and shelter from the elements. Scarcities and short-term disruptions in supply are a common phenomenon in many cities in developing countries as even the casual visitor can detect. Total failure of supply has been mostly limited to rural areas with drought as the chief culprit. This results in an enlarged flow of "ecological" refugees to the cities, thus adding to their burdens. So far, such major failures have been avoided in cities, although sometimes only by dint of herculean efforts and major expense. The threat remains very real however, and could be triggered off at almost any time.

(iv) Economic vulnerability refers to the possibility of financial loss or insolvency due to shock or changed circumstances or mismanagement. Thus if oil supplies are cut off or the electric power supply fails, there will be production losses in industries relying on such power source. More generally, the failure to achieve economic growth sufficiently rapidly in relation to population growth means that there is insufficient economic activity to provide adequate means of employment and income for large sections of the population, and insufficient national revenue to provide infrastructure and social services. Hence any sudden economic shock (a rapid rise in oil import prices; a dramatic fall in the world price for principal exports, e.g. minerals, food products) can plunge the nation into economic crisis almost literally overnight. The economic shocks of the 1970s has been met in many instances by heavy international borrowing, giving rise to the present debt crisis which threatens not only developing countries but the entire world financial structure.

(v) Functional vulnerability refers to the possibility of the failure or inadequacy of the organizational system. In its most dramatic form, this is the incapacity of governmental services to respond quickly and effectively to emergency situations. There is also a decline in the everyday functional capacity of governments to cope with problems associated with rapid urban growth.

Aggregate Vulnerability to Acute Events and Chronic Situations

The five types of vulnerability identified are interrelated. Deterioration in one area has a reactive effect elsewhere, so that the separation is somewhat artificial. It serves the purpose however of pointing to actions which are needed to reduce vulnerability. If measures of special and aggregate vulnerability could be devised, however arbitrary they may have to be in some respects, such measures would serve to identify priority areas where action is most urgently needed, and to indicate trends. There can be no doubt that the overall vulnerability of cities in developing countries is growing. But so too perhaps is the ability to respond — resilience. The purpose of this analysis of vulnerability and resilience is to identify ways of diminishing the former and strengthening the latter.

The relationship between events and chronic conditions is instructive. In imagining "worst possible scenarios" for cities in developing countries, it is sometimes proposed that they will collapse (Timmerman, 1981). The evidence of response to disastrous events seems to show that while there is little resilience in many developing countries, the international community still has both the sense of responsibility and the capacity to respond effectively as witnessed by the recent surge of assistance in the case of the Ethiopian drought, but the capacity of national and eventually international organizations to respond to crisis may be sapped by progressively increasing demands for routine assistance. Could some of the desperately overburdened cities in the developing world actually collapse? How close to collapse are the worst cases? What form might such a collapse take? Should we expect a sudden catastrophic end like the last days of Pompeii? Might the collapse be marked by the sudden withdrawal of a an occupying army or the invasion of hostile "barbarians"? Or is a slow lingering decline into ultimate death a possible fate? There is nothing but highly speculative answers to such questions at the present time. But to modify a well-known aphorism, we may say that "those whom the Gods would destroy, they first make vulnerable."

The Time Scale

Before moving to a consideration of responses to growing vulnerability, it is important to have a rather long-term perspective on what may be required. There is some reason to hope that the current pattern of demographic trends in the developing countries is following in the path of European and North American experiences. The underlying hope of all development efforts must be that sooner or later the developing world will achieve the demographic transition to a position of relatively stable population, with low birth rates, low death rates and long life-expectation. There are many signs that this transition is well underway and that birth rates and net reproduction rates will fall along with economic improvement and urbanization. Three recent estimates of future world population are shown in Figure 1. These each share the conclusion (perhaps assumption would be a more accurate description) that world population will tend to stabilize somewhere around the middle to the end of the next century. Depending upon assumptions of how, in fact, the demographic transition will be achieved, the total world population by then may be between 8.1 and 11.0 billion. If the proportion of the urban population in the world is eventually 50 percent, the absolute numbers of people living in cities will be between 4 and 5.5 billion. If the 80 percent figure

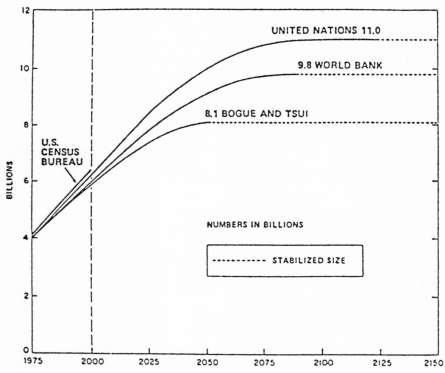

Figure 1: Three Predictions of World Population Stability

is attained, then world urban population will probably range between 6.5 and 8.8 billions (Table 2).

Most of this growth will take place in the presently less developed regions of the world. A pattern of human settlements on a world scale will probably emerge in which, of the approximately 7 billion urban inhabitants, 5 billion are living in the Third World. Can this transition be achieved without major disruptions to the global equilibrium?

A high rate of sustained economic growth in Third World economies based on a massive redistribution of wealth from the presently industrialized countries of the north to the developing countries of the south and improved conditions for the trade of Third World economies might achieve the necessary goals. Response on a scale commensurate with the growth of vulnerability in Third World cities is however not an immediate prospect. What then are present incremental policies and what can they achieve?

Response by Government and by Sector

The present "strategy" of dealing with the growing vulnerability of urban systems, (strategy is really much too dignified and important a term to apply to what is being done) is based heavily on response by government organized by sectors.

Since independence, developing country governments have assumed a large degree of responsibility for the planning and development of their own economies. It has been a common assumption that development must be stimulated, directed, even totally created by government intervention. Along with this philosophy has gone a growing caution about foreign investment by multinational corporations, and a relative neglect of small-scale indigenous entrepreneurs. Top priority has been placed on economic growth but this has commonly been sought by means of large-scale projects using foreign (governmental) loans. Factories of all kinds, roads, railways, other infrastructure and productive activities have been sponsored and funded by governments. At the macro-economic planning level, and at the level of construction, these policies have generally lacked either a spatial or an environmental component (Renaud, 1981). In consequence, they have tended to exacerbate some problems while contributing to the amelioration of others.

Thus it is a matter of the interrelationship between sectoral policies. Much the same is observed by Ministries of Health or Environment, which note that their effort at protection and improvement are being undermined by the policies of other ministries (especially economic planning and development) which are driven by other objectives.

This dominant response is perceived to have two major weaknesses at the present time. First, the sectoral react-and-cure approach to specific

Table 2: World Population and World Urbanization

Estimate of	Stable World Population (billions)	Urban population of world if 50% (forecast for 2000)	Urban population of world if 80% (as now in many developed countries)	Number of world urban population 1975	2000
United Nations	11.0	5.5	8.8		
World Bank	9.8	4.9	7.8	1.5	3.1
Bogue and Tsui	8.1	4.05	6.5		

problems is often so narrowly conceived that unanticipated, unintended and unwanted effects outside the policy domain (extra-domain effects) often combine to negate or even undermine and reverse the intended objectives of policy. Second, the assumption of sole responsibility by government agencies not only neglects, but frequently blocks, stifles and effectively prevents contributions being made by the private sector, including small-scale entrepreneurs.

Resilience or Reliability?

In thinking about measures to counteract the growing vulnerability of large cities in developing countries, it is helpful to consider the distinction between reliability and resilience. Reliability and resilience are properties of systems. Reliability refers to the capacity of a system to resist a shock or a perturbation without any significant departure from stable or equilibrium conditions. Compared with ordinary glass, the windscreen of a car has high reliability. It is so designed and made that if struck by an object at high speed, such as a stone thrown up from the road surface, the object will bounce off without damaging or changing the structure of the glass at all. Of course, reliability can be exceeded at which point the glass shatters.

What is true for windshields, reinforced concrete structures used in bridges and buildings, and the pressure vessels built to contain the reactor core in light-water nuclear generating stations, is also true for large systems such as electricity generation and distribution systems or whole urban systems. They are built to be resistant, but if the resistance levels or capacities are exceeded, they shatter and collapse.

The property of resilience, on the other hand, is the capacity of a system to absorb a perturbation by internal change and to bounce back to a stable condition. A trampoline or a mattress has resilience. Jump on it and it will yield to the pressure and later return to something close to its original state.

In thinking about the application of the concepts of reliability and resilience in the management of systems, three characteristics should be considered. First, there is a trade-off between reliability and resilience. It is not possible to maximize both simultaneously. Systems can be encouraged to develop in the direction of greater reliability or resilience. There is much evidence to suggest that human cities have been directed heavily, perhaps too heavily, towards reliability.

Second, resilient systems tend to be self-correcting. Impacted by a perturbation, they tend to "bounce back" without central direction or heavy external intervention.

Thirdly, reliability and resilience are concepts that have not yet been well operationalized and measured in complex systems. While the reliability of a pressure vessel may be measured, and the resilience of a trampoline, when it comes to complex interacting systems a detailed understanding of the way in which the system operates is required before it can be judged or measured in these terms.

Nevertheless, even lacking the precision of measurement, the concepts of reliability and resilience are useful heuristics in thinking about large complex human systems.

Let us describe the well-known Sahelian drought of 1972-75 in these terms. The savannah semi-arid grasslands belt that stretches across Africa on the southern margins of the Sahara desert has long been populated by nomadic and semi-nomadic tribes of pastoralists. Cattle are the mainstay of the economy and also play an important social role. The size of a herd is often a measure of the social status of a man and his family. The cattle also provide some insurance against periods of drought, when they can be sold off or traded for essential requirements. To colonial administration, bilateral foreign aid agencies and international development organizations, the availability of water appeared to be the main constraint on the growth of the pastoral economy and the improvement of the livelihood of the population. The human ecology of the Sahel was more resilient than reliable. When drought occurred, water sources dried up and cattle were sold or traded or sometimes died. A more or less stable equilibrium existed between human population, livestock and rangeland.

As a result of external intervention, programs of improvement were established which included as a major feature the drilling of wells. Such wells made the supply of water for cattle more reliable. Under the impact of such improvements, cattle herds grew in size and human populations also increased. When short droughts or periods of moisture deficiency occurred, the wells reliably continued to produce water. Cattle were not sold and did not die, but they did concentrate more heavily in those areas accessible to wells with resultant heavy overgrazing.

This process was greatly exacerbated in the severe drought of 1972-75. The perturbation was strong enough to cause many of the wells to run dry. The rangeland was overgrazed and the region could no longer support the population density of cattle and people that it had done previously. Many cattle died. Many people also died, either directly or indirectly as a result of the drought. A massive migration of the pastoralists also took place towards the more humid lands further to the south with some severe social conflicts.

The impact of the drought was so severe because the human ecosystem had lost some of its resilience. This loss was, at least in part, a direct result of the earlier gain in reliability.

The change became evident at the time of the perturbation, but its cause lay not in the drought itself but in the changes in the human ecological system which had extended over previous decades.

What is an appropriate management response to the drought? The initial humanitarian response was the provision by the international community of emergency food and other supplies. However successful this intervention (and it had many unpleasant aspects) it could not by itself restore the resilience of the local system.

After the emergency phase is over, the second response is to try to put a system back in place such that "this disaster will never occur again." The choice of action at this point is crucial. Usually the simple and obvious response is to make a substantial input of external capital and technical assistance to strengthen still further the reliability of the system. To do so may have many short or medium term benefits. It almost always reduces resilience and sets up a situation of high vulnerability to some future perturbation.

The recurrence of drought and famine conditions in Ethiopia, Sudan and other parts of the Sahelian zone in 1984-85 suggests that the response to the 1972-75 drought, however well informed, was not sufficient to create a functioning resilient system of human use. Indeed, the notion of "restoration" is clearly impractical. The pre-existing structure has been changed and it is pointless to attempt to return to the old equilibrium. What new stable structure will emerge is difficult to foresee at this time.

New Directions in Urban Management

The implications of this discussion of vulnerability, resilience and reliability for the urban systems of the Third World are considerable. A framework of thought is provided to examine management strategies for rapid large-scale urbanization. Much of the governmental intervention in urban systems management has had, and continues to have an air of "building reliability" about it. Considerable efforts are being mounted to prevent the breakdown of systems by enhancing their capacity to bear the pressures of mounting demand. Yet, as can be seen from the statistics of growth and the pattern of squatter settlements, the organized response is insufficient, and is slowly but surely being overwhelmed by events.

If the persistent conventional view of squatter settlements as "unwholesome, unclean blots on the landscape, symptoms of decay and a threat to orderly progress," is replaced by a view that sees them as elements of a new resilience, then indeed we may say that it is in these settlements that the new city of the Third World is being created. It is more appropriate therefore to call them "transitional settlements." They are stepping stones on the way to a new urban structure. Following this line of argument, possibilities for new directions in urban management are opened up. They do not however have to be "master-minded" by a central authority. Rather governments should consider best how they might create the conditions for the growth of resilient urban systems.

A good place to start is in the areas of what has been called economic vulnerability and functional vulnerability. The remarkable resourcefulness and ingenuity of squatters in finding or creating economic niches in the city has already been noted. So too has their capacity for self-organization. Migrants are adaptive people, often possessing an uncommonly high degree of enterprise and initiative. They have, by the very act of migrating to the city, already demonstrated this quality.

Governments can help by ensuring that "squatter" settlements have a proper legal status, that they have title to the land on which they squat and to the improvements which they bring about collectively or by households. Governments can also encourage and facilitate small-scale enterprise and entrepreneurship. They can help to strengthen functional resilience by reorganizing local organization at the community level and by not denying its existence or refusing to recognize community organization because it is not constituted according to existing legislation on local government.

Once economic and functional resilience are recognized and supported, there will be enhanced capacity to tackle other areas of vulnerability. Life support systems can be improved; structural vulnerabilities identified and removed, and biological vulnerabilities reduced.

There are innumerable possibilities for specific policy innovations and actions in these areas. They will depend upon careful working out of mutually understood and accepted responsibilities by governments (at national and local levels, with international assistance where appropriate) and self-organizing communities. Much can be done by the provision of technical information in a form that is usable by communities. Take for example the problems of house construction; control of insect and rodent disease vectors; the specific problems of child health, or the layout (plan) of building plots and access routes. In each of these areas, and in many others, technical information can be put to good use by local communities if it is presented as helpful guidelines for improvement rather than as a set of standards to which practice should conform.

Theoretical Perspectives

The growth of large cities and their present vulnerability can be viewed from two theoretical perspectives, both evolutionary. The first may be called Darwinian perspective and the second is associated with Ilya Prigogine and his theory of evolution through the self-organization of systems.

Darwinian or biological evolution proceeds at a very slow rate in terms of the human time-scale. Cultural evolution, in particular the development of science and technology, has accelerated the process enormously and has fundamentally changed the relationship of people to environment.

The wheel and the internal combustion engine have radically changed human power of locomotion. It is as though people had evolved much faster legs and grown powerfully effective wings. It is this dramatic evolution of what we choose to call "transport systems" that has enabled the large scale growth of cities to come about. But of course there are many more examples of technology substituting for biological evolution.

Telescopes and microscopes extend the power of the human eye, as does also television. Radio, telephone and now satellite communications extend the power of the human voice.

Large cities are one of the major manifestations of this techno-biological change, but are, of course, highly dependent upon the sustenance of the new technology. Human organization changes to exploit the technical possibilities. Just as the evolution of transport systems made large cities possible, so now the evolution of communications is rending such large agglomerations redundant. There are much less compelling reasons for urban concentration now than 50 or even 10 years ago. And so the mature industrial city may be seen to be beginning a process of disaggregation, at the very time when cities in the developing world are exploiting the technical possibilities of the transport system on a scale never before achieved.

Where does the balance of advantage lie between the forces of urban growth and urban decentralization in terms of vulnerability and resilience?

Prigogine proceeding from experimental results in non-equilibrium thermodynamics, has argued that evolution takes place in discontinuous jumps when systems are in "far-from-equilibrium" state. If these concepts in thermodynamics are applied to social systems, it is tempting to observe that Third World cities are not only growing in vulnerability but are also in a highly unstable state of disequilibrium. A bifurcation point has been reached (or is fast approaching) at which major restructuring becomes inevitable.

These theoretical perspectives seem to support the contentions that Third World urbanization is a new phenomenon representing an evolutionary step in the ecology of human settlements, and that being in a highly vulnerable state in far-from-equilibrium conditions, new structures can confidently be expected to emerge. A strategy of attempting to enhance the resilience of cities would appear to have the advantages of "swimming with the tide," and of helping to create conditions in which the new structures which emerge will be less vulnerable to the inevitable surprises that the future secretly holds.

Bibliography

B. J. L. Berry, 1981, *Comparative Urbanization: Divergent Paths in the Twentieth Century* (Macmillan Press, London)

K. Davis, 1969 *World Urbanization: 1950-1970* (University of California, Berkeley)

C. Dickens, *A Tale of Two Cities*, Numerous editions

C. S. Holling, 1973 "Resilience and Stability of Ecological Systems." *Annual Review of Ecological Systems*, Vol. 4, pp. 1-23.

William H. McNeill, 1977 *Plagues and People* (Penguin Books, Harmondsworth, Middlesex)

J. Mpinga, 1985 "Controlling the Chemical Threat" *The IDRC Reports* Vol. 13, No. 1, April 1985, pp. 20-22.

B. Renaud, 1981 *National Urbanization Policy in Developing Countries* (Oxford University Press, for the World Bank, New York)

P. Timmerman, 1981 *Vulnerability, Resilience and the Collapse of Society*, Environmental Monograph No. 1, Institute of Environmental Studies, University of Toronto

A. F. Weber, 1899, *The Growth of Cities in the Nineteenth Century* (Macmillan Company, New York)

H. Zinsser, 1935, *Rats, Lice and History* (Little, Brown and Company, Boston)

Comments on <u>Dimensions of a New Vulnerability:</u> <u>The Significance of Large-scale Urbanization in</u> <u>Developing Countries</u>

Members of the staff of El Colegio de Mexico

The author's vision of the process of urbanization on a world scale can be accepted "on its face value," although it poses some difficulties. However, it is felt that solutions based on self-construction in housing need to be based more on the abundant literature on the subject. On the other hand, there cannot be a world-scale strategy for dealing with the urbanization problem, not even on a regional scale; at most, on a national scale, due to the diverse conditions and prospects in Third World countries.

A stable relationship between rural and urban spheres must go hand in hand with a reduction of the income differences among sectors. There is no "linear" solution, as the author may seem to suggest. It is not enough to say that generalizations should be cautiously stated; the question is, how to deal with the diversity of conditions.

In any event, it would appear that to approach the urban management and development issues from the solution to housing problems would not be appropriate, but only a partial view. There is large diversity of situations, and families and individuals differ as to expectations and claims. Infrastructure must in any event be built: water, drainage, transport, health, environmental quality, etc. Small-scale enterprise is desirable; also the achievement of better and innovative relations between governments and governed.

Perhaps the author tends to give a rather catastrophic view of the future. The future is of course uncertain, but in the history of cities, we have always lived in a "far-from-equilibrium state."

3

The Heating Up of the Climate

John W. Firor
National Center for Atmospheric Research
Boulder, Colorado

The activities of people influence the biosphere of the earth in many visible ways. When forests are replaced by cropland, when grasslands are replaced by deserts, or when estuaries are dredged or filled, changes in the number and kinds of living species in the vicinity are easily observed. Impacts on larger scales are less easily identified.

The phenomenon of acid deposition, although surely involving human activity and biospheric changes, is much more difficult to describe with precision. And on the largest scale of all — the planet — changes occur slowly, impacts are subtle, and local human activities tend to obscure the effects of global activities. Nonetheless, human activity is today inadvertently producing a major change at the planetary scale — a warming of the earth's climate.

The activity consists of changing, slightly, through industrial and agricultural activities, the composition of the atmosphere by adding long-lived, infrared absorbing gases, such as carbon dioxide, methane, chlorofluorocarbons, nitrogen oxides, and substances that affect the supply of ozone in the lower atmosphere. These gases in the atmosphere absorb some of the infrared emission that would otherwise escape from the earth and return it to the surface, thereby increasing the temperature experienced by humans and most other living things. **A growing scientific consensus exists that some time in the next century the surface of the earth will become warmer than it has been at any time in human history.** This essay reviews the analysis that forms the basis for this consensus and outlines some of the policy issues that the warming presents for world leaders.

How the Greenhouse Effect Works

There is no controversy over the fact that the greenhouse effect operates currently in the atmosphere of the earth. This conclusion is most easily demonstrated by a very simple calculation. We know that the average temperature of the surface of the earth has changed very little over long periods of time, indicating that the amount of energy received each year from the sun and absorbed by the earth closely equals the amount of energy radiated back to space by the earth in the same time. Since we know quite accurately the intensity of sunlight arriving at the earth and the fraction of this light that is absorbed by the earth, we can compute what the temperature of the earth would be if it had no infrared absorbing gases in the atmosphere while other features of the earth-atmosphere remained the same. This temperature would be about -18 degrees Celsius. The actual average temperature of the surface is about +15C; so today the greenhouse effect is warming the earth's surface by 33C. Were this not the case the earth would be ice covered and a difficult place for human habitation, or indeed for humans to have evolved in the first place.

The basis for this simple calculation is illustrated in Figure 1. The radiation arriving from the sun, Q, is partly reflected by such things as clouds, dust particles, and light colored regions of the earth, and partly absorbed by the earth and atmosphere. The in-coming energy received by the earth is balanced by out-going infrared radiation. But infrared radiation from the surface of the earth has difficulty escaping directly to space, since much of it is absorbed by the various greenhouse gases now in the atmosphere.

Thus the bulk of the radiation that does escape must come from higher up in the atmosphere, from where it can easily penetrate the remaining air overhead. We know from the equilibrium calculation that the amount of this radiation that escapes is equivalent to that from a body at -18C, so we can approximate the situation by considering that all of the escaping radiation comes from the level in the atmosphere that is at -18C, shown on the diagram as Te, even though in fact some comes from higher and some from lower levels. Since the temperature of the air decreases as one goes upward towards the stratosphere, Te will be lower than the surface temperature, Ts. Thus the total radiation away from the earth, which is characterized by Te, is determined by the need to balance the in-coming energy, while the surface of the earth is much warmer than Te, as determined by the greenhouse effect.

Figure 1 also serves to describe the effect of adding more carbon dioxide or other greenhouse gas to the air. With more infrared absorption, the level from which radiation can escape the atmosphere moves higher to get above

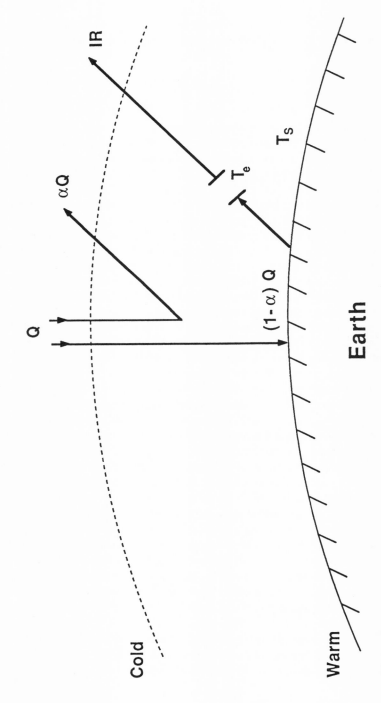

Figure 1

the added absorption. Higher in the air means colder, so the whole atmosphere and surface must warm to raise the temperature of that new radiating level to Te, or -18C, the value needed to balance the incoming sunlight.

Modeling the Greenhouse Effect

The simplest mathematical model of the globally averaged climate is based on Figure 1. With measured values for the incoming solar energy, the optical properties of the gases in the atmosphere, and the rate of temperature decrease with altitude, the size of the current average greenhouse effect can be computed rather closely.

It may seem from this that we could compute exactly how much the surface temperature would warm if the amount of carbon dioxide or other greenhouse gases in the air is increased. But difficulties arise. For example, the results of the calculation are very sensitive to the amount of water vapor in the air, since water vapor is also a powerful greenhouse gas, much more effective in fact than carbon dioxide. But if the surface air warms as the result of the added trace gases, it is reasonable to suppose that the amount of water vapor in the air will increase, since on a warmer planet more water would evaporate from the ocean and the air would be capable of carrying more water vapor. (This process can be seen to operate every year—there is on the average more moisture in the air in the summer than in the winter.) And if there is more water vapor, the surface will be made warmer still. To include this feedback process in the calculation requires a much more complex atmospheric model, one that goes into more detail than the one-step calculation of the average temperature over the earth.

The additional detail needed includes not only information about how much water vapor is added to the air but also how conditions differ from one place on earth to another. Radiation reflected or absorbed and the radiation emitted to space strongly depend on local circumstances.

The amount and kind and height of clouds, the color of the ground, the temperature of the ground or air, the presence of snowcover, all influence the local streams of radiation. And although the concentration of carbon dioxide in the air is very nearly the same everywhere, the amount of water vapor is highly variable and must also be related to location. Furthermore, water vapor, heat energy, momentum, dust, and other factors can be moved from one place on earth to another by winds and from one height in the air to another by convection, so the complete calculation of how the atmosphere behaves becomes very complex indeed.

The history of the study of the greenhouse problem has been one in which research scientists have attempted to add, one by one, the necessary features to their models of the climate. For example, the use of a single global average has been replaced by successively more detailed representations of the earth's surface; the single calculation of a temperature has given way to a calculation, hour by hour, of a changing weather pattern; and a long list of physical processes thought to be important have been included in the calculation. Today in these complex models, realistic winds develop, clouds form, move, precipitate, and disappear, air flows over mountains, moisture is exchanged with the ocean surface, soil moisture accumulates and evaporates, and snow and ice come and go with the seasons near the poles.

The fact that the models now encompass such a large fraction of the processes that we believe to be important in the behavior of the atmosphere suggests that the models are sufficiently realistic to provide guidance on the kinds of climatic change to be expected in the coming years.

But before such guidance can become useful, the realism of the models must be tested against known climate behavior. These tests, known as verification, fall into three main categories: comparisons of model calculation with current climate, comparisons with current climate change, and comparison with what we know about the history of climate.

Verification of Models

The simplest climate model can only be compared with the long-term average of the global temperature. But a sophisticated modern model should correctly predict the average temperature, pressure, precipitation, and other features, not only for the earth as a whole but at each location on earth. The model should also reproduce accurately the amount of year-to-year fluctuations around the averages. One can also ask whether the internal details of the model are correct, for example, whether the energy flows are of the right magnitude or the winds are correctly simulated.

The best of modern models survive these tests well enough to create confidence in their global results. Regional average climates appear much as observed and fluctuations are not unlike those that occur in the real atmosphere. (Some discrepancies remain in the internal workings of these models—the temperature of some layers in the high atmosphere are much too cold, for example.)

One interesting test which requires the models to incorporate conditions vastly different from those experienced on earth is to simulate the atmospheric parameters on Mars and Venus. Here, too, the models perform well, and in the case of Venus, which exhibits an extreme greenhouse effect, the agreement between model and observation is reassuring evidence of the realism of the underlying processes that drive the simulations.

But these static comparisons with today's climate cannot guarantee that the models will be realistic when used to foresee a specific, long-term climate change. So the model should also be compared with observed examples of climate changes. The most easily observed climate change is the change from summer to winter, and current models simulate this change with considerable realism. Not only is this change large and well observed, its cause — the movement of the sun north and south of the equator — is well understood and well described. That climate models can simulate this change increases our confidence in their reliability.

Phenomena that are not as well understood as the seasonal cycle are used to test models. The El Niño effect, or warming of the equatorial eastern Pacific Ocean surface, is associated with a characteristic pattern of weather over the North Pacific and North America. Although the cause of the El Niño is still in doubt, the best of current models give qualitatively the observed downwind climate pattern when the ocean temperatures in the model are changed in the appropriate way.

Another way to test the models uses information concerning climate change over thousands of years. Some rather well described changes in climate have occurred since the retreat of the last ice age, and the transition from ice age to our present interglacial was an even larger change. Astronomical theory and observational evidence point to the slow changes in the earth's orbit around the sun as an important cause of ice ages, and hence possibly of the smaller climate changes since. Climatic details of the last 18,000 years have been pieced together from various kinds of indirect or proxy information, and it is instructive to compare these data to the predictions of a model calculated for various times since the retreat of the ice began, using the earth orbital configurations that existed during that period. When these comparisons are made, some striking agreements are found, and these results serve to increase further the confidence that a useful degree of realism has been achieved in climate models.

Model Deficiencies

"Useful" is not the same as "accurate in every respect," and several deficiencies remain even in today's most complete models. The most troublesome weakness may be the way in which clouds are simulated. Clouds are, simultaneously, exceedingly complex and very important to the working of the climate (and hence of climate models). The amount of solar radiation reflected back to space is critically dependent on the amount of cloud cover, and the amount of infrared radiation from the top of a cloud to space depends on just how high in the atmosphere the cloud top is. But the formation and growth of a cloud or cloud system involves, among other things, such subtle things as vertical motions of the air, water vapor saturation, presence of nucleating agents, and vertical temperature structure of the air. Once formed, clouds affect radiative balances depending on cloud thickness, the size of water droplets, impurities in the water drops, and perhaps other quantities. Even the most sophisticated of today's climate models can only create clouds on the basis of a few, rather simple ideas; for example, whenever the model finds the relative humidity above a certain value it makes a standard cloud at that location. The difficulty of improving this aspect of atmospheric models is compounded by the fact that observations are not yet sufficiently comprehensive to reveal just what processes are most important in cloud formation.

These deficiencies in the way clouds are included in the greenhouse calculations however do not cast fundamental doubt on the conclusion that a warming will occur, but they create uncertainties in the projected magnitude of the warming and its distribution over the earth.

Computations for today's climate models are carried out on the largest computers available, ones that perform many millions of operations each second. Even so, to keep the calculations within the confines of available computing resources, the number of points used to describe the atmosphere are fewer than desirable, resulting in considerable blurring in the distinctions between mountains and plains, land and water, and ice-covered and open surface. For example one of the most elaborate climate models today uses about 1900 points over the surface of the earth, each point representing about 270,000 square kilometers.

One point must therefore represent the average conditions over all of England, for example, or all of Greece plus the Aegean Sea, or, in the United States, all of New Mexico from wooded mountains to white sand deserts.

Thus a second aspect of models that clearly needs improvement is spatial resolution. Larger computers now being manufactured should soon allow models with a much finer mesh of grid points to be calculated. The errors caused by the blurring of one type of surface with another, or by the improper accounting for the small scale motions in the atmosphere, can then be reduced.

Finally, the effects of the ocean cause considerable difficulty in climate models. A model that realistically incorporates all important atmospheric phenomena, with fine spatial resolution, will still be inadequate to deal with all features of climate change over decades or centuries unless it can be coupled with a suitable model of the oceans. Most of the surface of the earth is ocean, and this vast expanse of water can absorb and give off water vapor and heat; it can move heat from one location to another; and it is such a large heat reservoir that it can delay a change in climate for many years.

To describe the problem presented by the oceans we must review the manner in which greenhouse effects are usually calculated. The model is first adjusted to represent the atmospheric composition as it is today. The model is then integrated, or "run," for a long enough simulated time not only to allow the year-to-year climate fluctuations produced by the model to be reduced by averaging but to allow the atmosphere to come to equilibrium with the amount of infrared gases in the model atmosphere. Model results take the form of averages, such as the temperature during the summer season at a particular location or around a particular band of latitudes.

After such results are obtained for calculations using today's conditions, new results are produced with the model atmosphere modified to include more greenhouse gases — the usual change is to double the amount of carbon dioxide. Once again the model is run sufficiently long to insure that the model climate has fully come to equilibrium with the prescribed amount of infrared gases. These results are then compared with the previous run. It is from just these kinds of comparisons that the basic statement of the greenhouse problem arises: a doubling of carbon dioxide in the atmosphere will warm the surface of the earth by somewhere between 1.5C and 4.5C , more in the polar regions and less in the equatorial regions.

This experimental procedure keeps the concentration of infrared gases fixed at the current or doubled value during the run of several simulated years. But the amount of carbon dioxide and other greenhouse gases is changing continuously today, and is likely to be changing at the time carbon dioxide doubles. This would not cause any great difficulty were it not for the time lag in the greenhouse effect that will be produced by the large heat reservoir of the ocean.

The ocean-land distribution is very different in the southern hemisphere than in the northern hemisphere, so one can expect that the lag in warming produced by the ocean will also be different in the two hemispheres. This difference will produce changes in the general circulation of the atmosphere that could be major and which are not envisioned in the equilibrium type calculation described above. Equally troublesome is the possibility that the ocean circulation itself, which is driven by winds, rains, evaporation, and other interactions with the atmosphere, will go through changes as the atmospheric circulation evolves, and hence change such major features of the total system as the transport of heat away from the equator or rate of heat transfer to the ocean.

The other most notable uncertainty in the greenhouse calculation created by this lack of detail about how the ocean works is in projecting the regional manifestation of the warming. We know from studies of the small climate changes of the recent past that all areas do not warm and cool the same amount. During the first half of this century, when the northern hemisphere was warming a half degree, some midlatitude locations warmed four times that much and other locations cooled.

While it seems likely that a greenhouse warming will result in similar variations, we cannot today say what exactly the distribution will be. Complex greenhouse models are in general agreement on the size of the global warming and on the larger warming near the poles, particularly the margins of the Arctic Ocean. But the details of the warming in each region differ significantly. Similarly, these model experiments show increases in rainfall in some locations and decreases in others, but the agreement between different models on the rain distribution is poor. This limitation of models will not easily be removed until our understanding of many aspects of the oceans, such as the vertical mixing of heat down from the surface and the relation of ocean circulation to surface conditions, are improved. Even then, the simulation of transient effects will require long computer runs, perhaps 50 years of simulated time, using models with improved ocean simulation and with gradually increasing amounts of greenhouse gases.

Despite these remaining uncertainties, models today can alert us to future possibilities about the climate, and their realism is such that a projection of climate change must be taken seriously. That projection is: **if the concentration of green house gases in the atmosphere continues to increase as in the last 50 years, the climate in the next 50 years will become warmer than at any time in human experience.**

Increase of Greenhouse Gases

But will the concentration of greenhouse gases continue to increase as they have in the recent past? How much these gases will increase in the air depends on how and at what scale the world's societies continue the industrial and agricultural activities that release these gases to the atmosphere. Behavioral scientists, economists, and technologists are not yet able confidently to estimate trends in these activities in the absence of policy governing trace gas emissions, and no effective move toward global policy is yet in sight. The standard approach is to discuss this question on the basis of today's rates of change of greenhouse gases in the atmosphere, and then to speculate on factors that may modify the present trends. Each important greenhouse gas presents somewhat different issues.

Carbon dioxide, which was the first greenhouse gas to be recognized as such, has received by far the most attention. The concentration of carbon dioxide in the air a hundred years ago is estimated to have been between 260 and 290 parts per million, volume (ppmv), and measurements today give 345 ppmv with a yearly increase of about 1.5 ppmv or approximately 0.4% per year. The increase in atmospheric carbon dioxide is almost certainly due primarily to the use of fossil fuels in energy production. Coal is mostly carbon so that when it is completely burned the end product, in addition to heat, is carbon dioxide. Liquid and gaseous fossil fuels are hydrocarbons, so the gases resulting from complete combustion are water vapor and carbon dioxide. Thus carbon dioxide is a necessary end product of the full conversion of any fossil fuel to energy.

Various techniques have been employed to estimate the amount of coal, natural gas, and oil remaining in the ground. But what is known about the fuels that could be mined does not provide any useful limit to the amount of carbon dioxide that can be emitted — we could easily double or quadruple or eventually multiply by eight the atmospheric concentration with available reserves. So estimates of future emissions must focus on what societies will do about energy use. Different studies have produced quite divergent estimates of future fossil fuel use, ranging from a gradual decrease in global use to an annual increase of several percent. The current rate of increase is in the neighborhood of 2 to 3% per year; at that rate the carbon dioxide concentration in the air should reach 500 ppmv in the year 2020 or 2030 and 600 to 800 ppmv in 2060.

These numbers for future atmospheric concentrations are dependent not only on the rate of emission of carbon dioxide but also on the rate at which living things on land and in the ocean can take up this gas and convert it into some form that is stored away from the atmosphere for a long time. The ocean processes are not completely understood, so future projections of their influence are not settled. On land, the issue that has received most attention is the effect of deforestation and other land use changes on the carbon dioxide concentrations.

If a forest is converted into cropland, the carbon stored in the trees is eventually released as carbon dioxide to the air, either by the burning of the forest or the slower decay of the wood. Conversely, a new forest takes up carbon dioxide and stores it as long as the forest continues at the same level of total biomass. Recent work indicates that these phenomena will not be of major importance in future changes in the atmospheric concentration of carbon dioxide, but that they could have been important in the build-up that has occurred to date.

The uncertainties in the estimates of future carbon dioxide concentrations make it impossible to frame a statement such as the climate will be X degrees warmer by the year Y. The careful studies by economists of various scenarios of fuel use do, however, begin to give us a tool for policy analysis. If the high fuel use countries were to agree that it is wise not to risk a climate so different from anything in previous human experience and call for a ceiling to be put on the atmospheric concentration of carbon dioxide, these studies will be an aid in deciding at what rate the available options (switching, for example, to solar and renewable fuels, improvements in the end-use efficiency in the use of fossil fuels, economic incentives to reduce fossil fuel use, building more nuclear power plants) must be instituted to keep the concentration below the selected upper bound.

Each of the other greenhouse gases presents a different problem. The simplest one to study may be the chlorofluorocarbons (CFC's) which are used in refrigerators, spray cans, and some industrial processes. The two main representatives of this group of gases, CFC-11 and CFC-12, are presently increasing in the air at a very high rate, about 5% per year (compared to about 0.4% per year for carbon dioxide.) And unlike carbon dioxide, these gases have no appreciable interaction with living material or the oceans, they have no non-human sources, and they are manufactured entirely for a rather narrow range of industrial and domestic uses. Furthermore, since these substances were earlier identified as contributing to the harmful destruction of stratosphere ozone, they have already been the subject of international agreements and of specific controls in several countries. Hence they may present fewer, or at least different, obstacles to international policy attention than does carbon dioxide.

The most difficult gas to consider may be methane. This gas gets into the atmosphere mostly from anaerobic decay of biomass, in swamps, rice paddies, or in the digestive systems of cattle and termites.

Some methane escapes from natural gas wells and pipelines or from coal deposits; a small amount is a byproduct of some industrial processes. Methane is removed from the air by reactions with the hydroxyl radical. The concentration of methane in the air seems to be increasing at 1 or 2% per year. The cause of this increase is unknown but speculations include such things as the increase in rice production, the increase in cattle production, the rising number of termites in the tropics, and the competition for the hydroxyl radical by carbon monoxide released from automobiles and industry. Thus many uncertainties surround methane.

Nitrous oxide, another greenhouse gas about which there is much uncertainty, is also a complicated product of biological activity. The use of nitrogen fertilizers in agriculture may be behind the increase observed in its concentration in recent years, but it is not certain. Nitrous oxide concentration is currently increasing in the atmosphere at a slower rate than methane.

These are the major greenhouse gases emitted to the air by some mechanism and now known to be increasing in concentration. One more gas must be mentioned, however: tropospheric ozone. Ozone is created in the lower atmosphere by a complex set of chemical reactions. It is most famous as the gas in the high atmosphere that absorbs ultraviolet light from the sun, thereby reducing the amount of sunburn humans experience. But ozone also absorbs infrared light effectively, and so, in the lower atmosphere, it is a greenhouse gas. It is thought that the average concentration of this gas is increasing in the lower atmosphere. If this increase is anthropogenic, it is likely due to releases to the air of nitrogen oxides and hydrocarbons — products of a wide range of industrial and agricultural activities, from driving cars to raising livestock. These gases add to the reaction chains that create ozone and so increase its concentration in the lower atmosphere.

It is obvious that it is more difficult to comment on the possible future concentration of methane, nitrous oxide, and ozone than it is for CFC's and carbon dioxide. But if we foresee the kinds and magnitude of impacts the human-induced climate change can produce, some sort of projection of future emissions is needed. In particular, we would like to know whether, with emissions and resulting atmospheric concentrations that are well within reasonable limits, large climate changes could occur. In order to make such a projection we can take the present rates of increase of these gases (but using lower values for CFC's, since it seems unlikely that the very high current rate of 5% per year can go on for long) and compare their calculated effects with that for carbon dioxide, assuming that fossil fuel use continues to go up at its present rate. The total warming so computed is about twice that for carbon dioxide alone!

What is a Large Climate Change?

The range of global average temperatures that has occurred since the retreat of the last ice age and the beginning of settled agriculture seems to have been within plus or minus one degree of the average.

The thermometer was only invented a few hundred years ago, so this number was not measured for most of this period but must be deduced from other information. A variety of approaches give similar results and add confidence in the estimate that deduced climate changes were associated with average temperatures varying within this range.

It is possible to study the impacts these "one degree" climate changes have produced. Historians and geographers study this question and argue vigorously about it, since it is rare to find a situation in which people are experiencing climate change when no other features of their society are undergoing rapid evolution. But it is clear that a one degree change is a large one. Perhaps the most striking example is the comparison of the warm Eleventh Century A.D., when Norse sailors explored the North Atlantic and left settlements along the coast of Greenland, and the "Little Ice Age" a few centuries later when these settlements vanished under meters of ice. The same span of time saw the decrease in rainfall in the American Southwest from amounts just capable of supporting small agricultural communities to much dryer conditions. So even a one degree change can have a major impact on climate-sensitive societies. We have no prior experience at all of a climate shift several times larger. Yet it appears that, if present trends of emissions to the atmosphere of several gases continue, the earth will be several degrees warmer within the lifetimes of people already born.

Policy Responses

It might be thought that the prospect of such a rush into unknown conditions would have galvanized leaders the world around to slow the process and allow a more careful exploration of the new conditions.

That this has not happened is of course due to the difficulty of slowing anything so basic to the current world civilization and economy as fossil fuel use and food production. People would rather hope that the projections are wrong. This situation— apparently essential activities leading to a possibly unacceptable change — has led to a careful examination of each of the steps in the process of projecting a warming to see if these calculations are unnecessarily alarming— perhaps some aspect of the climate system will automatically limit the degree of change, or perhaps some overlooked feature of the ocean or the biosphere will stabilize the amount of carbon dioxide, methane, nitrous oxide, and ozone in the atmosphere.

So far the more we learn the more critical the situation appears. Early simple models that showed much smaller warmings have been found lacking in critical aspects and have now been superceded by vastly more complex and careful accounting for known effects in the atmosphere.

Feedbacks in the climate system have been found to be mostly positive, that is, they make the response larger, as in the case of the snow-ice feedback. This feedback is a sequence of causes and effects in which the initial warming causes a melting back of the ice and snow line toward the poles, which uncovers earth, darker than snow, thus increasing the heat absorbed from the sun and so producing further warming.

Similarly, ocean chemical and biological studies have revealed no process that will strikingly speed the uptake of carbon dioxide; in fact deposits of methane complexes at the bottom of shallow seas raise the possibility that a warmer ocean may emit methane and so heat the earth even more. Some plants will grow faster with additional carbon dioxide in the air, but the annual cycling of most plants means that this effect will not store large amounts of carbon dioxide away from the air. Some plants will need less water if the carbon dioxide in the air is higher, but this will be balanced in many places by the greater evaporation of soil moisture due to higher temperatures. In summary, the vigorous search for reasons not to be concerned about the greenhouse effect has so far failed.

The appropriate strategy for us to take in light of this situation has been described by many writers. The main elements are:

1) take those steps that slow the emission of greenhouse gases, giving more time for adaptation; and

2) initiate the process of adaptation to a changed climate by taking reasonable scenarios of climate change into account in future plans.

These writers have also pointed out that many of the steps recommended are beneficial to society even in the absence of a climate change, so the costs of slowing, or getting ready for, a major climate warming will be less than might be anticipated. For example, improved economic and social organization are needed now in some countries to prevent recurring droughts from triggering famines, and these steps will also ameliorate the impacts of climate change. Further, if we are able to slow the coming of the warming, using less fossil fuels must be at the center of our strategy. But in the developed world, fossil fuels also cause acid rain, urban smog and carbon monoxide, and in some cases, severe national balance-of-payments problems.

Improving the end-use efficiency of fossil fuel energy, or replacing fossil fuel with other sources, therefore has much to recommend it in the high-use countries, even before one considers the greenhouse issue. Leaving these additional benefits aside, however, and taking the greenhouse problems alone, actions of the following kind are most frequently proposed:

Decrease the use of fossil fuels in the developed countries.

Improve future increases in fossil fuel use in the developing world by emphasizing energy systems based on renewable resources, and other sources.

Improve efficiency of energy use everywhere.

Decrease the use of long-lived chlorofluorocarbons.

Search for explanations for the increases of methane, nitrous oxide, and ozone.

Improve models to give reliable outlooks on the local and regional manifestations of the global change.

Improve irrigation systems and agricultural research and development to increase resilience to climate change.

Build regional food reserves and other forms of flexibility into each country's plans.

These steps, if taken promptly, may be enough to allow a smooth transition to the incompletely understood, but surely different, climate likely to be experienced in the next century.

Comments on <u>The Heating Up of the Climate</u>

Members of the staff of El Colegio de Mexico

This is a clearly stated presentation of the current theories used to explain climatic changes. However, he does not mention the effect of a cooling due to reflection of short waves by the atmosphere, due to natural causes (volcanic eruptions), to industrial emissions, to increasing particles due to erosion and so on. The 'nuclear winter' discussion is also relevant. The document might also discuss certain ideas put forth which seem to contradict Firor's position, even though he would not accept them. It also seems important to give some idea of the timespan involved in warming of the atmosphere vs. cooling processes.

Responses to Comments on __The Heating Up of the Climate__

John W. Firor

Elbek overemphasizes the role of the opposition to nuclear energy in producing the climate warming. He is correct that a more rapid growth in nuclear electric generation capability could replace some coal use, but we know today that carbon dioxide is only part of the problem. The chlorofluorocarbons, methane, nitrous oxide, and tropospheric ozone are increasing in the atmosphere and can result in a climate warming irrespective of whether the growth in carbon dioxide slows or not. So the precise rate of growth of nuclear power is of interest, but is not the overriding factor in the climate change.

But he is certainly correct that international negotiations to reduce coal use would be difficult. Perhaps the best approach is the one mentioned near the end of the paper — let's do those things, such as gain an increase in energy end-use efficiency, that should be beneficial in any case. It may be that steps such as this one can be accomplished without attacking head-on the thorny issues of who is to blame for the current concentrations of carbon dioxide in the air or whether there will be winners as well as losers as the climate warms.

The comments from El Colegio ask for more discussion of possible cooling effects and of ideas that contradict those in the paper. There are three kinds of cooling that have been discussed over the years as relevant to the greenhouse warming: volcanos and other dust sources, ice ages, and negative feedbacks in the climate system. It is believed that a volcanic eruption that puts large amounts of sulfur dioxide into the stratosphere can produce a global cooling for a period of a year or so. These eruptions occur more or less randomly, and their effect are already incorporated into what we regard as the climate of the past. Thus they will have no averaged influence on the warming discussed here, unless they happen more often in the future, at an accelerating rate to keep up with the greenhouse gases — a very unlikely event and not one we should count on in making plans for the future. Some years ago it was speculated that just as human activity was emitting carbon dioxide and warming the climate, that same activity was placing dust in the air which would counteract the warming. Studies since have shown that the total amount of dust in the air is not increasing, and that even if it were, its effects would warm the earth in some places and cool it in others rather than produce a universal cooling. An extreme source of particles in the air would be fires following a nuclear war—the so-called nuclear winter or nuclear autumn problem.

It is important to note that the same atmospheric models used to predict a greenhouse warming are the ones used to calculate the effect of such intense injections of smoke and dust into the atmosphere. The difference is that the greenhouse effect is much closer to normal conditions than is nuclear winter, and more details of the green house calculation is likely to be more nearly correct than the nuclear winter one. Thus if one accepts the proposition that the nuclear winter scenario should influence national and international policy, one should be even more certain that the greenhouse calculations are worthy of action.

Our current understanding of ice ages indicates that they are triggered by small changes in the earth's orbit around the sun. Since we know the earth's orbit quite well, at least for times of tens of thousands of years, we should be able to estimate when the next cooling spell will begin. These estimates involve a thousand or several thousand years, as contrasted with the several decades that will pass as the earth warms by an easily measurable amount. So the two effects do not cancel.

I am not certain what are the ideas referred to that contradict those in the paper. The history of the study of the greenhouse effect is filled with ideas about some other effect that might slow, cancel, or even reverse the warming trend. But as suggested in the paper, these have failed to survive close scientific examination. One of the most difficult problems has been the role of clouds. As the climate warms, more water will evaporate from the oceans, more rain will have to fall to balance this evaporation, so there is a possibility that there will be more clouds on a warmer earth. More clouds will reflect more sunlight, thereby reducing the warming. Calculations of cloud amounts are still one of the more controversial features of climate models. The best modern opinion is that the uncertainty in the cloud effect could be large enough to produce a factor of two error in the results; that is, if carbon dioxide is shown by the model to warm the globe by 3C, the uncertainty due to clouds may make this value as small as 1 1/2C or as large as 6C. Since 1 1/2C is large enough to take the world outside of climates experienced since the retreat of the last ice age, and since the gasses other than carbon dioxide will approximately double the carbon dioxide greenhouse effect, this uncertainty due to clouds does not change any of the discussion in the paper.

The instrumental records of the global temperature have also been seen by some as indicating that the greenhouse effect is not taking place. From 1880 until 1940, temperatures on land in the Northern Hemisphere generally warmed. But then from 1940 through 1970 these same locations cooled, causing many to wonder if something were wrong with the greenhouse theory. More recent data collections have shown that:

1) the Southern Hemisphere warmed steadily throughout this period, and
2) the Northern Hemisphere resumed its upward trend in 1970 and has reached the highest average temperatures ever recorded early in the 1980s.

The existence of some unknown effect that can cause average temperatures to wander up and down by a degree several times in the last ten thousand years requires us to be cautious in interpreting any temperature sequence of only a hundred years. So the most that can be said of this record is that it is consistent with, but does not prove, a long term, greenhouse temperature increase.

There is one other idea that is sometimes cited as counteracting the greenhouse effect. This one is called the Gaia Hypothesis, in which it is speculated that all living things work together to maintain the climate of the earth within a livable range of temperature. This hypothesis has not yet been developed so that it can begin to be tested against observations. But even if it is later proved to be applicable to the climate on the earth, it does not say the climate will remain as even as is desired by modern industrial and agricultural societies. We know, for example, that during the Cretaceous period in geological time the climate was much warmer than at present; polar ice caps were small or vanished completely and plants that cannot endure freezing temperatures grew in what is now central Asia. It was also a time of lush biological activity—great forests, dinosaurs, and more. So clearly living things did not maintain anything like today's conditions, and such occurrences as a greenhouse warming of several degrees, melting of the polar ice, and a sea level rise of a hundred meters are not ruled out by Gaia.

4

Greening of the Desert

Amos Richmond

The Miles and Lillian Cahn Chair in Economic Botany
The Jacob Blaustein Institute for Desert Research
Ben Gurion University of the Negev
Sede-Boqer, Israel

Introduction

Greening of the desert, which implies conversion of many arid regions into lands that support a standard of productivity equal to or surpassing that of today's more humid areas, represents one of the greatest challenges confronting the family of man. The future thus may witness an intensive development of many of the Arid Lands which today provide their inhabitants with only a meager existence. While entire deserts cannot be transformed into pastureland and forests, and desert development into thriving habitats will be confined to selected areas, I wish to propose that the next century will witness a significant exodus into today's drylands.

Humanity, by that time, will have relieved itself considerably from the present burden of dependence on fossil fuels, and will be producing abundant energy from essentially unlimited resources. With the application of economic methods for water desalination on the one hand and the development of plant production systems based on using brackish and sea water on the other hand, sweet water will cease to be the limiting factor in the development-potential of the arid zones.

Indeed, new plant species and new biotechnologies that will be particularly suitable for the special desert environment will create a point of attraction for both people and capital. Time will then be ripe for transforming large tracts of lands in the perpetual sunny, warm, dry and barren areas into blooming and thriving habitats. Then the wide open spaces that often form a unique and beautiful landscape, and the clear, dry air that could mean comfortable living throughout the year, will be recognized. Many dry lands of today will be in great demand for the homes of tomorrow.

First and foremost, however, the reclamation of the dry lands will provide livelihood and security to many of today's impoverished natives of the arid zones.

Viewed from this standpoint, greening of the desert is at present essentially a moral issue. It is the obligation of the more prosperous people living in the more humid, highly productive regions to assist their fellow human beings, natives of the dry lands who at the present are doomed, with few exceptions, to poverty and to malnutrition which all too frequently becomes starvation. Indeed, nearly all the centers of deprivation on our planet are in the arid regions, in which poverty stemming from population growth and low productivity of the land is accentuated by fluctuations in the limited amount of water that is available. As distances on our globe shrink rapidly, whenever a part of humanity is exposed to severe misery, its fate is communicated the world over. Starvation thus can no longer be ignored without threatening the moral fiber of those who look at the other side.

Accelerated population-growth results in an ever increasing number of 'environment refugees' (1), thus 'greening of the deserts' carries obvious political ramifications: The deprivation prevailing today in the dry lands could, if accentuated, threaten world peace. The cumulative hostility of the starving "have nots" may erupt in a manner that will endanger the mutual well-being on this globe. Thus ethical consideration, as well as self-interest, formulate the thesis that increasing the productivity of arid lands represents a goal of utmost importance and urgency for mankind.

The Desert Ecosystem and Human Ecology

The life of all organisms, man, animal and plants, depends on the harmonious interaction between themselves and their biotic and abiotic environment. Organisms and environment together form an organic whole, a community for which the term 'ecosystem' was coined and which can be minute or can be large, covering the entire globe. Evolution through natural selection, has created ecosystems in which composition, structure and function of all the biotic components are in a dynamic equilibrium with their natural environment.

This natural state of affairs changed when man started to develop agriculture and began to live in large population centers. Today, the population explosion in many arid lands is accompanied by increasingly larger urban and industrial centers with their unavoidable pollution of air, water and soil. These as well as over-exploitation of the biotic environment, are destroying whole ecosystems, damaging others irrevocably and in some areas even threatening man's existence (2, 3).

The arid zones are most sensitive to processes which disrupt the equilibrium in the ecosystem, and, yet are most responsive to the limiting factor — water. This is elucidated in the description of the desert ecosystem which follows.

The desert ecosystem

Desert areas are defined as such on the basis of the moisture available, which is a reflection of the amount of precipitation and the potential of evapotranspiration. As a rule desert lands are dry, but there cannot be an exact measure with which to distinguish between desert and non-desert areas. Another typical feature of the desert is the scarcity of life which is expressed in both the small number of biological species and the low population density. But for the limited forms of life, the desert ecosystem is in many ways no different from other ecosystems and it cannot be sustained without an inflow of energy to the system and within it.

However, while in other ecosystems, the overall quantity and range of available energy flow form the limiting factors which mold its nature, the desert ecosystem is limited by the amount of available water. Thus, the rate of energy taken up and utilized could have been much larger if more water was available, and the same is true for the energy flow within the system (3,4).

An effective rain event activates biological processes, in particular production and reproduction, resulting in a build up in biomass of plants and animals. The average annual net above-ground primary production varies between 30 and 200 g/m2 in the semiarid zone (4). This production exhausts the ration of available water supplied by the rain and after a usually short growth period, water becomes limiting and both growth and biomass sharply decrease to a steady state.

Water moves in the system through essentially the same compartments and paths as energy and carbon. Indeed, the water-controlled nature of arid ecosystems is essentially due to the tight coupling of energy inflow with water outflow. Noy-Meir (5) points to an important property of water as a limiting factor in an ecosystem; like energy, but unlike most nutrients, water is not recycled in the system but cascades through it. This is because the amount of water returning from plants and animals back to soil is negligible, relatively little evaporated or transpired water is recycled locally. Clearly, water is essentially a non-cyclable, periodically exhaustible resource, replenished only by new input.

Three aspects of the water flow system should be stressed: (a) the overall quantity of water that reaches the system is small; (b) unlike the supply of energy which is essentially constant, water is supplied irregularly, in varying quantities and in time intervals which may be very large; (c) of all the environmental factors that affect the desert ecosystem, the supply of water is least predictable, being the factor with the highest random value; and for the larger life-forms, some spatial concentration of limited water supplies is essential. Indeed, since the appearance of water is of such a random nature, reproduction in the desert ecosystem became quite opportune, being usually expressed only if and when the system had sufficient water.

Spatial variation in rainfall is a distinct feature of the desert ecosystem, being one of the causes of patchiness in desert environments. It affects both species diversity and the adaptive behavior of organisms. Low spatial correlations mean that at a time of draught in one locality, there is still a fair probability of favorable conditions in some other part of the region, of which mobile organisms can take advantage.

Thus, the control of population size in the desert ecosystem becomes unique. Unlike species which live in a more stable environment and in which internal controls to regulate the population density have evolved, population size of desert organisms is greatly dependent on environmental factors and thus varies greatly. Under unfavorable conditions, no reproduction occurs at all, whereas under good conditions, very prolific, non-controlled reproduction takes place. 'Population Explosion' is usually eliminated in desert species by the fact that favorable environmental conditions are only temporary, followed by much longer periods which are unfavorable for existence. Thus, the major problem faced by desert species is not reproduction, but more basic – the security of mere existence (4).

According to Noy-Meir (4,5), man faces in deserts the same problems of the water-heat-salt balance as any mammal, but has hardly developed special physiological adaptations. In general, humans have a certain capability for acclimation to extreme temperatures. However, even populations with some physiological characteristics which might be of adaptive value to life in the desert need to drink almost every day. Nevertheless, man has occupied most arid zones since the hunting-gathering stage, essentially by behavioral adaptations.

Mobility enabled man to adapt a strategy of nomadism whereby he could use water and food resources when and where they became available within a larger area. Two basic types of nomadism can be distinguished. One type is opportunistic, i.e. – the movements do not follow a fixed trajectory in time and space, a pattern which usually occurs in zones with erratic rainfall. Another nomadic pattern is cyclic or seasonal, in following a more or less fixed annual cycle which presumably attempts to optimize the utilization of food and water resources. This type of nomadism takes place where climate variations have a predictable seasonal component. Hunter-gatherers in arid zones have been reported to utilize almost all digestible sources of plant and animal food. In general, the diets of hunter-gatherers in arid zones is much more vegetarian than in other environments.

The effect of the neolithic revolution in arid regions of Asia and North Africa was thus essentially a transition from nomadic hunting-gathering to nomadic pastoralism, with supplementary and opportunistic crop growing in favorable sites (4). This meant a transition from direct utilization of a wide variety of energy sources to maximal diversion of energy flows for preferred domestic herbivores, allowing a great surge in population density. The greatly increased water requirements of human and stock populations that followed were partly met by the developments of wells and cisterns.

Several ecologists have argued against sedentarization of resources in an arid environment. While this may be true for stable populations, the only way in which man can increase food production and self-supporting population densities is by massive enhancement of primary production. Indeed, the many irrigation works that have been established throughout the ages and particularly in recent times in many arid lands bear evidence that arid zones may become enormously productive.

Ecological Aspects of Desert Settlement

Man, by this creative manipulation, modifies his surroundings and disturbs the existing natural balance. Land cultivation, grazing, construction, mining, industry and finally weather modifications, all represent different levels of man's interference with the environment (6). What is not always realized is that the natural balance in the arid and semi-arid region is most delicate, becoming easily and irrevocably destroyed.

The delicate and "fragile" nature of the arid and semi-arid ecosystems is of immense importance in considering desert settlement. Clearly, an inevitable conflict exists between the developers, whose major aim is to use the land for some end deemed worthwhile, and the environmentalists whose major concern is to guard the environment, foreseeing the toll that society eventually pays for a single-goaled orientation.

In any event, disregard to the ecological system, whether because of shortsightedness or ignorance, will cause society to pay a heavy toll for robbing its environment. As pointed out by Owen (7), many ecologists shun the fact that no matter how well arid zone natives, pastoralists and cultivators, seem to be adjusted to their arid environments, it is no longer correct to insist that their life styles cannot and should not be changed. In reality, changes are fast and long-distance trucks, instead of camels, now cross deserts such as the Sahara. Cultivators in arid Africa are learning about cash crops and technological innovations have been filtering the remotest areas. Yet governments and social leaders must realize how pollution of the environment or careless exploitation of natural resources may create disasters of frightening and painful magnitude.

A point at hand are large areas in Africa, which until recently supported cultivation or livestock, and which now have become unproductive deserts. Indeed, there is little disagreement that desert-like conditions are expanding at an alarming rate. As became clear from the United Nations Conference on Desertification, held in Nairobi in 1977 (8), there was little disagreement that desertification was largely the result of human activities, for the evidence of a climatic change that causes the decline in rainfall is rather poor or altogether missing. In that conference, it was claimed that 600 million people living in arid lands are at risk from food shortage as a result of desertification and that of these, one tenth are in imminent danger. The recent drought-induced famine in Ethiopia and the Sudan bear this out.

The major causes of degradation of the desert ecosystem have been identified by Larmuth (9), as follows:

(a) the breaking of new ground, particularly with mechanized assistance leading to profitable crops for a short time before erosion leaves the soil unsuitable for further use and the area is abandoned;

(b) overgrazing (and trampling) resulting in edible plant species becoming rare and the ground cover of long lived species being reduced, with consequent degradation and increased run off of scarce rainfall;

(c) removal of woody plants for firewood, often by pulling up the plant and thus damaging the root system and/or preventing further growth.

For the combat of desertification, an integrated "community ecology" approach is needed according to Owen (7), the aim of which should be to determine sustainable carrying capacities which minimize the effects of drought and hold desertification. Of special interest in holding the process of desertification is the stabilization of shifting sand dunes, improvement of pasture around water holes and the development of shelter belts to conserve vegetation, range conservation through the use of firebreaks, methods for conserving rainfall, regulations for controlling nomadic movement and the reorganization of land use and village settlement (10).

Although many of the Middle East's and Africa's desert societies were primarily nomadic, great cultures developed and flourished in many desert regions in which the inhabitants developed agriculture and industry and learned to make use of their limited resources. Such knowledge, the fruit of long years of human experience, should be considered in research aimed at developing a concept for living in the desert which will be compatible with a modern style of living. It should be genuinely responsive to man's needs for physical comfort, aesthetic surroundings and social intercourse in the special environments (6).

Practical Aspects for 'Greening' the Desert

Until the recent introduction of technology, human sustenance in most arid regions was limited. Indeed, the desert had always been a marginal land, the inhabitants of which were living with the constant danger of famine. Nevertheless, in some limited areas, man had long learned to exploit favorable local conditions, using available water resources to create a basis for a secure livelihood. As already alluded to however, many examples are known from the past to our time in which, through population growth resulting in overexploitation, the natural resources were gradually destroyed, causing havoc to entire civilizations in the past and a substantial increase in the number of 'absolute poor' (11), today. The situation in the Sahel region south of the Sahara as well as in Ethiopia is a current example. Clearly, a lesson that emerges from the past is that in the final analysis, man's fate in the arid regions depends on his ability to refrain from irreversibly altering the delicate ecological balance (2).

Today, man's confrontation with the desert is growing rapidly. A new fabric of interrelationships is emerging and man should no longer be helpless when faced with the wide desolate spaces. Technology is bringing water, power and resources to places that hitherto spartanly supported very few. No doubt these developments will affect, with time, a far-reaching psychological and sociological metamorphosis for many of today's desert dwellers. As a matter of fact in some parts of the world, extensive and successful settlement of the desert is already a reality. One familiar example exists in the Nile Valley, which has been cultivated for millinea by the wise and able Egyptian farmer who has learned, throughout the generations, the most important of all in arid zone settlement i.e. – how to exploit the land for crop production without harming the delicate ecological balance. Modern examples for 'desert engineering' can be seen in West and Southwest USA, Australia, China, the USSR, many Arab countries and Israel.

There is thus ample practical evidence to demonstrate that with the aid of science and technology, it is possible to take the unique features of many arid lands – which untapped spell low productivity and little hope – and exploit them in such a way as to convert many desert areas into a thriving land that supports a good standard of living.

This anticipation should nevertheless not overshadow bitter experience and a sober truth which is now generally recognized, that technology in itself, when simply imported from one place of the world to another, is no guarantee for the betterment of life. Science and technology provide of course, only hope, not instant progress and in the lands to be reclaimed, very much depends on the comprehension of social justice and understanding, as well as on political unity and resolve.

The basic philosophy that was adapted by successful ancient agrarians should guide the modern endeavour of "greening the desert." Essentially, it entails development of production systems and strategies with which, on the one hand, the unique environmental conditions of the dry lands may be skillfully exploited, and which on the other hand—do not harm the fragile ecological equilibrium.

In this frame of reference, the following basic approaches will be considered: the exploitation and management of local water resources; introduction selection and genetic improvements of plant crops that tolerate drought and saline water and of animal species that are well adapted to the environment; and finally, new biotechnologies to grow plants and animals, based on sophisticated exploitation of brackish or sea water and of the unique environmental features characteristic to the dry lands.

(a) Exploitation and Management of Water Resources

The exploitation, management and application of local water resources represent a key issue in the development of arid regions. The basic sources for locally available water in many arid lands are run-off; ground water, temporary streams, cloud seeding and water desalination, as follows:

1. Water harvesting from run-off

An exciting story of reclaiming the desert by the ancients which formed the basis for a civilization that developed in the desert, is revealed by the ruins of six ancient cities situated in the foothills and highlands of the Negev Desert in Israel. Innumerable remains clearly indicate the existence of extensive agriculture dating back to the Israelite period (about 950 to 700 B.C.) and the Nabatean and Roman-Byzantine periods (about 300 B.C. to 630 A.D.). Clearly, even though these ancient cities were established as caravan towns to serve important trade routes and agriculture having thus a secondary function, many regions in the area were once intensively cultivated and supported a thriving civilization.

If however there has been essentially no significant climatic change in the last three thousand years, how could the ancient farmers have cultivated the land under a 100 millimeter or even 200 mm average annual rainfall without any source of additional water for irrigation? It took Michael Evenari and his colleagues many years of intensive efforts to answer this question (2). Their investigations revealed, first of all, that all ancient agriculture in the Negev foothills and highlands was based on the utilization of surface run-off from small and large watersheds; hence they referred to this agriculture as "run-off" farming.

When rain starts falling, it first hits the vegetation which prevents some rainwater from reaching the soil. In many deserts, however, this factor is negligible because of the scantiness of the vegetation. The first raindrops thus reach the ground and infiltrate the structureless soil in a slow rate. Whenever the rate of rainfall is greater than the rate of infiltration, part of the rainwater will fill the surface depression, and when the depression storage has been filled, run-off starts. The amount of run-off is in many cases mainly determined by the rate of rainfall on the one hand and the infiltration rate on the other hand. The infiltration rate, in turn, depends much on physiochemical qualities of the soil: In the Negev, the loess soil, because of its composition, forms a thin crust on its surface after being soaked. This crust is almost impermeable to water, affecting run-off at a rather small, i.e. circa 15 mm of rainfall.

The relationship between rainfall and runoff was thoroughly investigated by Evenari and his colleagues (2) who found that about 30 millimeters of an annual rainfall of 80 millimeters will cause runoff, 50 millimeters of an annual rainfall of 100 millimeters, and about 90 millimeters of an annual rainfall of 150 millimeters. The actual runoff collected depended on the size of the catchment. The largest catchment (350 hectares) produced only about 2.5 millimeters of runoff with an annual rainfall of 100 millimeters, a smaller catchment (10 hectares) produces about 13 millimeters for the same rainfall, and a very small catchment of 0.1 hectares (a "microcatchment") produces about 50 millimeters of runoff with the same rainfall.

Thus Evenari's conclusion was that the smaller the catchment the larger the percentage of rainwater which appears as runoff. Or, the smaller the catchment the larger the amount of runoff per unit surface. There is however an additional advantage to microcatchments. Rains which are ineffective, that is, do not cause runoff on the large catchments, are effective on the microcatchments. During one rainy season there was only one large flood on the 350 hectares catchment area but 11 floods on the microcatchments (2, 12).

The ancient farmers used various methods to collect runoff, the most common and successful of which were used in runoff farms that received their water from relatively small watersheds. Each farm consisted of two parts, the farm proper (that is the cultivated area) and the catchment basin. Each cultivated area was situated in a narrow valley bottom on loess soil, 1-2 meters deep, terraced by low stone walls. The farm's catchment basin (20 to 30 hectares in size) was on the surrounding slopes. When a rain occurred heavy enough to cause runoff, it was collected in channels that led it to the various terraces of the farm proper. The terrace walls kept part of the water standing on the field, where it slowly soaked into the ground. The surplus went through drop-structures in the terrace walls to the next lower terrace. The water harvest from the catchments averaged 150 to 200 cubic meters per hectare per year and since the ratio of cultivated land to catchment area in the farm units was more or less the same (1:20 to 1:30), one hectare of cultivated land collected runoff from 20 to 30 hectares of hillside catchment. This meant that each hectare of cultivated land received on an average about 3,000 to 6,000 cubic meters of runoff water per year. One to five floods could be expected annually, producing enough runoff to soak the loess soil of the cultivated farm area (2, 12).

An important aspect of the researches of Michael Evenari and his colleagues is that it carried a clear, practical message: large desert tracts today can be made to produce vegetation by utilizing flood water, requiring little capital investment. Indeed, there is sufficient evidence that in many arid lands, runoff agriculture can be used to produce field crops, fruit and shade-giving trees as well as pastures. The most promising crops in Evanari's constructed Avdat and Mashash farms were found to be pistachios, almonds and olive trees.

Reconstruction of some ancient runoff farms in the Negev demonstrated that runoff could be used to augment and recreate pastures in arid areas. It thus seems reasonable to believe that by using runoff methods in different variations, together with planting and sowing of the most effective pasture plants, the carrying capacity of suitable arid lands for grazing animals can be significantly increased. Indeed, on a given size area which carries one sheep, several could be maintained if flood waters and selected pasture plants were to be properly used. A point to stress in this context is that cultivation of shade-giving trees and grasses based on runoff water may also be effective for recreational purposes.

2. Exploitation of ground- and floodwater and its application

Aquifers containing fresh and brackish water have been found underneath many arid regions the world over. One well-researched example is the Nubian Sandstone, a thick, predominantly sandy sequence composed mainly of fine to coarse- grained sandstones (13). This sandstone aquifer extends all along the Northern margin of Africa, from Egypt through Libya to the western Sahara. A. Issar and his colleagues (14) estimate the quantities of water stored in this aquifer at a few hundred billion cubic meters under the Sinai and Negev deserts alone and suggest that although only a very small fraction of this water has pumpage potential today, this aquifer may develop to become of great economic importance. In Libya, this aquifer is already well exploited. The present arid climate of the area, the distances between the possible recharge areas and the areas where the water is found, as well as the large volume of water in storage, indicate that a large part of the water in this aquifer is fossil.

The age of the water based on the 14C dating method, ranges between 13,000 years to more than 30,000 years. The O18D2 ratios of this water are characteristic of precipitations in more temperate climates than the present one. In certain localities, however, this water could be brackish, containing five to ten times the quantity of salt that fresh water of average quality contains (14). For certain crops, this water may not be suitable without some desalination, but much of this water could be well used to grow salt resistant crops in well drained soils, or in closed systems and in algal and fish ponds. In addition to ground water, flood water may occasionally occur in the arid zones, in which most streams are dry except for the brief rainy season, when they fill with sudden flash-floods that run off rapidly to the sea. Interception of these waters can provide a useful addition to the water supply potential. The flow of these streams, fed by seasonal springs and supplemented by occasional flash floods of very high peak discharge, may be spread over recharge areas located in the coastal sand dunes, from where it can infiltrate and recharge an underlying aquifer.

A method that rapidly expands the use of brackish water and increases the productivity of the arid lands in general is trickle irrigation, which is based on the concept of applying water in small amounts over a long period of time. The technique consists of laying a plastic tube of small diameter on the surface of the field alongside the plants and delivering water to the plants slowly but frequently from special emitters along the tube. The concept, which is now called trickle or drip irrigation, has proved to particularly useful in arid areas (15).

If used to supplement chemical fertilizers, this method has beneficial effects on crop growth, overcoming most limiting factors for plant growth in hot arid lands. The constant supply of nutrient ions to the soil complex in the vicinity of the roots offsets the difficulties caused by the soil's coarseness of texture and deficient organic content. The frequence of water application to the root system has a beneficial effect on plants under stress because of dry weather conditions and/or hot winds. Insects attracted to the cultivated area can be eliminated more easily on unwetted plants. Finally, a major benefit of drip irrigation is that it facilitates the utilization of brackish water for crop production. This is because when irrigation is done with saline water, the concentration of salt in the soil increases as the soil dries out between applications of water. At such times the soil moisture tension rises, making it difficult for the plants to extract the remaining irrigation water from the soil. Salts gradually accumulate, and plant growth and crop yields decline. With drip irrigation, the buildup of salt is controlled by what is effectively continuous leaching. Salts are pushed out to the periphery of the root profile by an advancing front of water emitted from the orifices of the tube. The roots are able to take up water freely from the middle of the wet zone, where soil-moisture tension is low and the salt level remains nearly the same as it is in the irrigation water, a state to which plants respond with improved production (16).

There is thus convincing evidence that drip irrigation is a particularly promising technology for arid zones in helping to solve shortages of agricultural productivity by improving the efficiency of irrigation and facilitating usage of brackish water.

3. Desalination of brackish and sea water

In principle, desalination could provide sweet water in many deserts, turning them into green lands and revolutionizing the pattern of primary production on our globe. No method, however, has yet been invented that would desalinate sea-water at a cost that is not totally prohibitive for agricultural production. Nevertheless, the desalination of brackish water, which may have the salt content of 1/5 or 1/10 of sea water, may not be so far off for limited economic purposes, if the water will be used in closed or protected areas, where evapotranspiration is significantly curtailed. One promising method is based on the use of noncellulosic membranes for reverse osmosis (RO), which has been known for many years as a potential process for solute-solvent separation and started its great leap forward towards practical application with the discovery of the asymmetric cellulose acetate membrane.

The method, however, is not yet widely spread, for cellulose acetate membranes have several shortcomings. Some researchers believe that the simplicity of the RO process, the fact that most maintenance problems encountered could be eliminated by good engineering practice and, above all, the fact that RO is the desalination process with the lowest energy requirement, all combined to make it an attractive and promising desalination process (17).

Another promising method for water-desalination is based on energy extracted from a solar pond (18) which is based on simple basic principles: A black-bottomed pond exposed to solar radiation heating up by absorbing the solar heat. Normally, the water at the bottom is then heated, and rises by convection to the top, and the heat is dissipated. In the non-convecting solar pond, convection is suppressed by imposing a density gradient on the pond, made of salts at various concentrations. Because of the density gradient, it is possible to 'decant' the hot water from the bottom of the pond without disturbing the density gradient above the extracted layer. Calculations show that between 20 and 25% of the incoming solar radiation can be collected from the bottom of the pond providing energy for water distillation.

4. Rainfall enhancement

Cloud seeding in order to enhance rainfall has been experimented with in many countries for the last 25 years. Studies of cloud physics which were conducted in conjunction with the seeding projects have contributed greatly to the understanding of, and confidence in, the interpretation of the results, which are subjected to a careful statistical analysis.

The conclusions were that on practically all rain days, good conditions existed for the application of ice crystals to induce the formation of additional solid precipitation particles. This is because the relatively cold winter continental clouds had a low ice content and a high liquid water content. The increases in precipitation due to seeding were mainly attributed to effects produced in clouds that otherwise would not have precipitated. Also, seeding affected the formation of a more efficient prolonged rain process in clouds that were already precipitating naturally. A "dynamic seeding" technique, in which pyrotechnics of silver iodine are released into cloud tops, has been used with great success in Florida. If clouds over arid lands prove to have the correct proper ties, rainfall enhancement may prove an additional source of water enrichment.

(b) New plants and animals by introduction and selection

Selection of new crops tolerant of drought and soil salinity for cultivation in arid regions is still in the early stages, but research and experimentation has produced some promising results, some examples of which shall be briefly described:

1. Jojoba (*Simmondsia cinesis*)

The Jojoba is a hardy shrub, native to the southwestern United States and northern Mexico. Its seeds contain a liquid wax that seems to have an impressive industrial potential (19). The plant tolerates extreme desert temperature and thrives under relatively low soil moisture conditions which are not suitable for most agricultural crops.

A rainfall of 500 mm is sufficient to support productive stands of Jojoba well, but even 100 mm may produce a light crop and the plant has been known to survive as long as a year with no rainfall at all. It requires water during winter and spring to set its flowers and seeds, and its summer water requirements are low, in contrast to most summer crops which need most of the water when it is most scarce.

Jojoba also appears to be fairly salt-tolerant, one tested variety showing no detrimental effect on growth or production at a soil-water salinity of about 7,000 mg per litre. In loamy loessial soils with a rainfall of 200 mm Jojoba may be grown commercially without irrigation, attaining its full yield potential after 7 or 8 years. When precipitation is lower, irrigation is essential. The yield of Jojoba varies greatly in individual plants and yields as high as 5 kg per plant were obtained from selected plants (20).

2. Guayule (*Parthenium orgentatum* Gray)

Another example of a promising desert shrub of seeming important industrial potential is the Guayule shrub. This shrub grows in desert regions of north-central Mexico and south-western United States. All parts of the shrub contain rubber, which when purified is virtually indistinguishable from rubber from *Hevea* trees. A potential source of rubber for arid lands, it may be grown in poor desert soils.

To obtain the rubber, the whole plant is harvested, sliced into small fragments, macerated, and the lighter rubber is floated away from the vegetable residue. Yields of up to 12% (dry weight) have been obtained from wild plants and over 20% from improved varieties (21).

Still another crop of seemingly promising potential is the buffalo gourd (*Cucurbita foetidissima*), which tolerates extreme drought (22). Experiments indicate that the buffalo gourd could well match the performances of soybean and peanuts in well-watered lands (23).

3. Forage crops

Experience in various arid lands in the world indicate that the carrying capacity of the land can be significantly raised in many arid regions by enriching the flora through the plantation of annual forage crops. Largely through the efforts of M. Forti (24), much information is available on forage crops suitable for areas with up to 200 or 250 mm of rain in Israel. One of the most promising species is *Cassia sturtii*. Family: *Leguminosae*, is a shrub from the arid and semi-arid regions of southern Australia, which has demonstrated satisfactory year-round palatability. It has good grazing resistance and the leaves have a high protein content of about 12%, and annual dry matter yields (in two grazing periods) of about 1,000 kg per ha in a 200 mm rainfall area (24, 25).

Fodder plants of great potential are the "saltbushes" of the genus *Atriplex* (family: *Chenopodiacea*) They are highly salt-tolerant, and many are perennial shrubs that remain green all year. They make useful forage in arid zones of the world. *Atriplex nummularia* for example grows well in deep soil with only 200-250 mm rainfall. It extracts salt by forming small salt-filled bubbles (vesicles) on the leaf surface. When full the vesicles burst, releasing the salt to the wind.

The nutritive value of *Atriplex nummularia* and *Atriplex ha limus* is high: both have a digestible protein content averaging 12% of the dry matter (about the same as that of alfalfa). With only 200 mm of rainfall, these two species have produced about 8 to 10 times more than a good native pasture produces under the same conditions. They have survived (but without reproducing) a 12 month period with only 50 mm rainfall (24).

The spineless cactus (*Opuntia spp.*) is another fodder crop of great potential for the 100 to 200 mm rainfall areas. Spineless cactus possesses the exceptional characteristics of being able to store large quantities of water in the succulent parts. Aptly called 'camels of the plant world', these cacti can benefit from a shower of only a few mm, which would ordinarily be of no value to conventional fodder crops (26).

The jojoba, buffalo gourd, salt bush, spineless cactus, and guayule illustrate the great potential in systematic plant-introduction, which involves import of plants from any arid land around the world and testing their performance in a particular arid region. The most physiologically-adapt species would then be further selected for economic performance. This promising field is yet greatly unexplored. Norman Myers (23) mentioned the Aborigines in Australia who have been gathering a great many drought-adaptable plants, favoring certain yams, well adapted to dry conditions. Likewise, the yeheb nut bush from Somalia (*Cordeauxia edulis*), as well as a marine plant from the west coast of Mexico (*Zostera marina*) could be successfully introduced to many dry lands.

Similar to plant-introduction, introducing animals which are better adapted to 'desertified' areas represents an approach of promising potential. One apt example is the camel, which could beneficially replace cattle and goats in many arid lands. The camel can provide milk under conditions in which other ruminants may barely survive. Camels could thus conceivably improve the food supply in several hunger areas throughout the arid world (39).

4. Tree selection for afforestation:

The need for tree plantation in arid regions is rather obvious. Trees are used for controlling soil erosion along wadies, and for checking wind erosion and sand dune expansion. Of particular importance in barren lands is the supply of shade and improvement of the landscape. Finally, the wood itself is in great demand.

Observations in experimental plots over many parts of the arid region in Israel have revealed that two genera are particularly adaptable to arid conditions – the Eucalyptus and the Acacia, other successful trees being certain species of Pine (*Pinus*), *Melaleuca, Dodonea, Pistacia, Prosopis, Tamarix* and others (27).

Thirteen different species of Eucalyptus were found suitable, including *E. cacaldulensis var. subcinerea*, which was particularly tolerant to calcareous soils, and *E. clelandii*, which was well-adapted to sandy soils, but the best performance was exhibited by *Eucalyptus occidentalis*, The other species which performed very well in the observation fields were Acacia, two species of which - *A. salicina* and *A. cyclops* - were most successful.

These observations show clearly that flood water can be used most advantageously for afforestation. Indeed, along the high ways in the Negev highlands several flood catchment areas have been constructed and planted mostly with species of Eucalyptus and Acacia.

The use of novel approaches may well accelerate progress in selection of plant crops and trees suitable for arid environments. In recent years, plant geneticists and plant breeders have been using, at an ever-increasing momentum, techniques which are commonly regarded as "bioengineering." Likewise, it is possible to envisage new hybrids of animals, to produce organism, both terrestrial and aquatic, which could better yield in dry lands as well as in sea- or brackish water.

Plant tissue culture has become in particular an essential complement to plant selection and breeding, replacing tedious and time-consuming field work (28). These techniques open up many fascinating possibilities for the development of new plant species adopted to arid environments. It is, e.g., possible to remove the walls of plant-cells and fuse the protoplasts to make new hybrids. Many tissue-culture methods can be used in connection with DNA hybridization, one possibility being gene ration of vectors that facilitate the transfer of individual genes between chromosomes of unrelated species (28). Another interesting possibility offered by tissue-culture techniques is the creation of "artificial seeds" (29), which may be so designed as to permit the delicate emerging seedling a better change in coping with a harsh environment in its early stages of development.

Summing up, there is to date ample tested information concerning strategies and tactics by which to augment the food production potential of many arid lands. The future seems even brighter.

(c) Biotechnologies for warm Deserts

Brackish water provides the basis for revolutionary biotechnologies, designed to exploit the unique desert environment, e.g. algaculture as well as plant and fish production in closed systems. These technologies shall be described in some detail in what follows.

1. Controlled environment agriculture

The main disadvantage for cultivation of plants in hot desert regions is that the lack of fresh water is coupled with a very high evapotranspiration potential. In addition, pronounced seasonal and diurnal fluctuations in temperature are often harmful. Nevertheless, the same arid land characteristics also offer definite benefits. The most striking is a high level of annual solar radiation which in many areas exceeds 8300 m-joules per square meter, over twice that of northern Europe. Some other characteristics of desert regions which are of potential advantage are high daily winter temperatures and the availability of brackish water.

From a practical standpoint, a "closed" environment is a greenhouse in which some of the solar energy and a good part of the water are conserved and in which there is only a limited and controlled exchange of the gaseous environment inside with the outside air. As pointed out by J. Gale, the challenge in the development of closed-system agriculture is how to optimize the environment for plant growth at an acceptable cost (30).

Saving in water use represents one obvious advantage in closed-system agriculture. Other advantages, include the possibility of adding CO_2 to enhance growth and the heating of the plants at night using heat accumulated during the day. An added advantage to closed-system agriculture in the desert is that in an environment of high humidity and moderate temperatures, the resistance of any plant species to saline water is increased. Consequently, locally available brackish water may be well used for closed systems, especially if diluted with solar-distilled water.

Under field or greenhouse conditions, once the soil is completely covered by a crop, transpiration accounts for almost the entire water expenditure. When the rate of water loss exceeds that of uptake and transport to the leaves the stomata close. This reduces vapor loss but also the uptake of carbon dioxide. Under the conditions of a closed-system, air humidity is high, wind velocity is low thus plant water use is only about one fifth to one tenth of that of a crop growing in an open field in an arid region, which is particularly high. Furthermore, the farmer will need only about 1/20 of the area to make his living from high-value cash-crop greenhouse-type farm, than from irrigated open-field agriculture.

There are still many difficulties with the system. Excessive leaf temperature is one of the cardinal problems of closed-systems in arid regions. In addition, several plant diseases may arise in a high-humidity atmosphere. A major problem in closed-system agriculture is the establishment of a favorable energy balance. This requires capture and storage of surplus daytime solar energy and its release to the greenhouse at night. The same heat storage system should be used in the summer months for dissipating surplus energy.

There is a large number of possible engineering approaches to the capture, storage and release at night of surplus energy from the day-time period. The systems being studied at the Institute for Desert Research in Israel by a group headed by J. Gale are based on the liquid optical filter principle. This type of greenhouse exploits the fact that only about 48% of the solar radiation (in the 400-700 nm waveband) is used by plants in photosynthesis.

The remaining U.V. (É nm) and near infra-red (700-3000 nm) are not directly used by plants.

The greenhouse is being built of a hollow, 6-12 mm thick, essentially transparent plastic roof. Water is circulated through this roof to a tank which serves for heat storage — (either directly or via a heat exchanger). A dye is added to the water, which then absorbs the U.V. and near-infra-red but transmits the 400-700 nm waveband. In this way about 50% of the solar energy is prevented from entering the system. However most of the 400-700 nm waveband is also transformed to heat within the greenhouse, which must also be removed. As the roof is held at a temperature a few degrees lower than that of the plants, heat is transferred to the roof by convection, conduction and to a small extent by long-wave radiation. A further important contribution is condensation, on the roof, of water transpiring from the plants. This runs off and is collected and returned to the plant roots. In this way excessively high temperatures are prevented during the day. At night, due to the low air temperatures prevalent in arid regions and consequent net loss of long-wave radiation, the greenhouse tends to cool rapidly. This is prevented by recycling the stored warm water through the roof or through pipes that heat the root system, increasing the resistance of the foliage to chilling. Initial calculations have indicated however that, in the hottest hours of the day during the summer season, some ventilation will be unavoidable to enable cooling by latent heat dissipation, at the expense of water use.

Carbon dioxide fertilization to increase productivity is a potentially important feature of closed-system agriculture. According to Bassham (31), adding CO_2 to a continuously-harvested alfalfa crop would result in a theoretical maximum production of 200 tonnes/dry weight per hectare, annually. He suggests that, with appropriate closed-systems and protein extraction technology, this may prove to be a means of producing protein for cattle, poultry and humans in desert regions.

One possible way to supply the fresh water requirements would be by desalination solar-stills of available fossil brackish water. Solar stills are only marginally economical and under certain well-defined conditions; however, it seems that they may be an ideal source of fresh water for closed-systems in desert areas because of the high solar irradiance and low cost of land. An important advantage is the intrinsic linkage between the rate of production in solar distillation and the rate of water demand in closed-system agriculture. Both rates depend directly upon solar radiation. Furthermore, since under closed-system conditions (high humidity and CO_2-moderated temperatures) plants have been found to exhibit increased resistance to salinity, fresh distilled water may be mixed with brackish water to increase the overall yield of water suitable for plants in the closed-system.

2. Production of algal biomass

Detailed description of the many facets of biotechnology of algaculture has recently been published (32,33).

Algae are aquatic plants which range in size from large multi-cellular oceanic species over 30 m in length down to microscopic unicellular forms, comprising several thousand species which may be grown under a wide range of conditions. Algae production represents an extreme approach in modifying desert conditions for the growth of plants, but the general concept is plain: it calls for the use of the high rate of solar irradiance and the high temperatures prevalent in most deserts throughout the year, coupled with locally available saline or even sea water, i.e. water not suitable for the production of most useful land plants, to grow algae. Conditions and resources which are in effect limiting to growth and development of conventional agricultural crops are conducive to the growth of many algae species, conferring a specific advantage on algaculture in hot arid zones. Indeed, one species, the cyonobacteria *Spirulina platensis*, is indigenous in Lake Chad, in the Sahel and has been collected from the lake and used as a food supplement by the natives in that region.

In addition to their tolerance of saline water, many species of algae have other distinct advantages over conventional agricultural plants. Algae can be grown in a continuous culture, continuously absorbing the maximal rate of solar irradiance and the entire plant body of the alga is harvested and used. Also, all nutrient requirements can be maintained at the optimal level making it possible to maintain growth conditions in which there is no nutrient limitation. Therefore in an intensive, correctly maintained algal system the only limitations to growth may be environmental, i.e. temperature and light. When nutrients and temperature do not limit growth, production becomes limited by light and when the system is light-limited, the output is greatly affected by the population density, and by the extent of turbulence in the pond as has been explained.

Commercial systems for the mass cultivation of algae relate to several technical aspects, e.g., the construction of the pod, its shape, depth and system of mixing the algae-laden water, the type of lining. Also, the separation of the algal mass from the medium and its dehydration represent major technological issues, the satisfactory solution of which is essential before large scale cultivation can be economically pursued.

Usages for algae: The most obvious usage of algae is as animal feed and as a human food supplement (34). The food potential of certain microscopic algae has been fairly intensively studied in the past few years. The blue-green alga *Spirulina* belonging to the family *Oscillatoriaceas* is particularly interesting. Rediscovered by the academic world as recently as 1940, *Spirulina platensis* has been collected from the salty lakes and ponds along the northern shores of Lake Tchad since time immemorial, sun-dried and eaten by the Kanembou people. *Spirulina geitleri* was apparently used in a similar fashion by the Aztecs at the time of arrival of Cortez in Mexico. Spirulina is an easily harvested, multicellular filamentous alga of high digestibility and mild flavor which has been found to contain up to 70% protein of good nutritional quality. The quality of protein from the green alga *Scenedesmus obliquus* has also been thoroughly investigated. Considering any international nutrition parameter, *Scenedesmus* and *Spirulina* compare very well with most common animal feeds such as soybean extract and fish meal. The high content of proteins found in microalgae makes this product a concentrate by itself, having a significant advantage over conventional vegetable sources of protein, which usually have a much lower protein content.

The nutritive value of *Spirulina*, as well as of many other algal strains, is amplified in that it has a relatively low percentage of nucleic acids (4%) compared with bacterial protein. The mucoproteic membranes that separate the cells are easy to digest, unlike the cellulose cell wall found in many other nutritional algae. It is completely non-toxic, its lipids being made up of unsaturated fatty acids that do not form cholesterol, perhaps making *Spirulina* suitable food for patients with coronary illness and obesity.

Preliminary conclusions from experiments with Carp and Tilapia are that algae are very well accepted by these and other fish. Significantly, microalgae contain a high quantity of carotenoids, important for intense soloration of shrimps and certain species of fish.

The possibility of using algae as a human staple has been researched in the past decade. A significant insight was provided by the work of Hernandes, Gross and Gross, who investigated the effect of *Scenedesmus acutus* powder as a food additive in Peru (35). Their thesis was that the high protein content, as well as iron, vitamin B complex and carotene, along with considerations of previous positive tests on humans, made this powder an interesting product for combatting protein-energy malnutrition and vitamin deficiencies.

Protein is only one of several products which can be commercially derived from algae. There are various chemicals which are already extracted from algae and others which are envisaged as becoming commercial products. Today three major algae products are extracted from marine algae, i.e. alginic acid derivatives, carrageen and agar. Alginic acid is extracted primarily from seaborne microalgae — *Laminaria* and *Microcystis*. The alginates are used for various purposes for example in the food, cosmetics, textile and rubber industries.

Algae may be grown in very high saline mediums. One interesting example is *Dunaliella*. The possibility to culture it commercially is currently being investigated. *Dunaliella* may live in the Dead Sea where salinity is ten times higher than it is in the ocean. Production of glycerol is essentially the means by which this remarkable adjustment takes place – and, when exposed to extremely saline medium such as exists in the Dead Sea, the glycerol content in this algae may become as high as 75% of its weight. A product of much greater value of this algae is B carotene which is provitamin A and in addition is used as a food dye. Some species of *Dunaliella* may contain as much as 10% of their weight in B-carotene (36).

At present, algaculture is still far from providing a source of inexpensive food and chemicals. Mass production of microalgae outdoors is a formidable task. Much more remains to be learned about the biology involved in this biotechnology and many technological details must be improved. Production procedures have to be simplified and the average annual yields have to increase severalfold before algaeculture can become a significant agricultural endeavor. Nevertheless, the promise of cultured algae, particularly as a salt-tolerant crop in warm and arid lands, is real.

3. Intensified controlled fish growth in tanks

One possible way for optimal use of water resources in warm deserts is by intensified fish growth in controlled systems (37). This may be accomplished by raising a high concentration of fast-growing warm water fish in small volume tanks. The fish tank wastewater could in turn be treated, recycled and reused. Also, the water for many species of warm water fish could be brackish, of low alternative usages.

The advantages of growing a fish culture in tanks were described by Oron *et al,* (38). First, limited amounts of water can be used to obtain fish growth comparable to that obtained in conventional artificial fish ponds. Secondly, increased fish biomass loading (LD; kg fish/m3 water) can be utilized. Under regular conditions, and with a polyculture, LD is around 2 kg/m3 , whereas under intensified, controlled and mono-culture conditions, LD may be raised to 15 kg/m3 or more. Finally, decreasing the size of the fish growth system minimizes water losses due to evaporation and seepage, thereby improving water conservation. This is further achieved by recycling the fish tank waste-water by one of many possible methods (38).

In Summary

Is greening of the desert economically feasible? Based on learned intuition, the various schemes and tactics described here represent in principle economically sound targets. Indeed, it is my conviction that this endeavour is not a pipe dream or science fiction, but is definitely possible. It requires a genuine belief in the importance of this mission and perhaps even a farsight as to its profitability in the long run. Basically, 'greening of the desert' is a scientific and technological endeavour and requires cooperative efforts by many inter-disciplinary groups of scientists and engineers. Indeed, very much needs to be researched before the economics of arid land development can be analyzed in some detail. It is nevertheless clear, in my opinion, that significant improvements, albeit far from being fully satisfactory, can already be economical, this assertion being based on the technological know-how and experience available today.

Finally the matter of education needs much careful attention. The gradual elevation of arid lands to higher productivity requires a vast social and economic adaptation. Education must be provided to facilitate coping with an expanded economic and social complexity which will accompany a sophisticated transformation of the arid environment. Thus an integral requirement of any plan that concerns improvement in arid regions is a significant broadening of education without which the "taming of the desert" could not proceed. In other words, an economic system based on more sophisticated means to harness environmental factors so as to achieve unique modes of productivity, requires a relatively high standard of technological education. Thus the educational aspect which must accompany schemes for greatly increased productivity in arid lands would become perhaps the most important bonus in the course of our efforts to "green the desert."

References

1. El-Hinnawi, E. Environmental Refugees. United Nations Environmental Program, Nairobi, Kenya.

2. Evenari, M., Shanan, L. and Tadmor, N. The Negev, Harvard University Press, Cambridge, Mass. 1971.

3. Safriel, U. In: *The Desert: past, present and future.* Ed. E. Zohar, Reshafim, Tel Aviv, 361 pp. 1977 (In Hebrew).

4. Noy-Meir, J. Desert Ecosystems: Higher Trophic Levels. *Ann.Rev.Ecol and Systematics* 5, 195-214, 1974.

5. Noy-Meir, J. Desert Ecosystems: Environment and Products. *Ann.Rev.Ecol. and Systematics* 4, 25-51, 1973.

6. Richmond, A. Research Priorities and Organization for Arid Zone Development. In: *Arid Zone Development; Potentialities and Problems.* Eds. Y. Mundlak and S. Fred Singer. Ballinger Pub. Co. 1977.

7. Owen, D.F. Drought and Desertification in Africa: Lessons from the Nairobi Conference. *OIKOS* 33, 137-151, 1979.

8. United Nations Conference on Desertification. Desertification: An Overview. -A/CONF.74/1 (Mimeograph)

9. Larmuth, J. Desert and Man: A Future? *Third World Quarterly* 1(3), 104-111, 1979.

10. Rapp, A. Regional studies and proposals for development: Sudan. In Rapp, A., Le Hourerou, H.N. and Lundholm, B. (ed), Can direct encroachment be stopped? *Swedish Nat. Sci.Res. Council Ecol. Bull.* 24, 155-164, 1977.

11. Anonymous. The State of the Environment. United Nations Environment Program. Nairobi, Kenya, 1985.

12. Evenari, M., Nessler, U., Rogel, A. and Schenk, O. Fields and Pastures in Deserts. Information and Consultation: 6111 Heuback Erzbergerstrasse 16, Bundesrepublik Deutschland.

13. Issar, A., Rein, A. and Mitchaeli, A. On the Ancient Water Resources of the Upper Nubian Sandstone Aquifer in Central Sinai and Southern Israel. *J. of Hydrology*, 17, 353-374, 1972.

14. Issar, A. Water in the Negev. Groundwater in the Negev. In: *The Land of the Negev,* Part I. A. Shmuewli and Y. Gradus. Ministry of Defense, Tel Aviv, 1979.

15. Kobe, S. Drip Irrigation, *Scientific American*, 62-68, Nov. 1977.

16. De Melach, Y., Pasternak, D. and Twersky, M. Drip irrigation, a better solution for crop production with brackish water in deserts. United Nations Conference on alternative strategies for desert development and management. Sacramento, Calif. U.S.A., May 31, June 10, 1977 (Mimeographed).

17. Glueckstern, P. and Greenberger, M. Technological and Economical Evaluation of Various Reverse Osmosis Units. *Seawater Desalination*, Proc. 11th Nat. Symp. on Desalination. Eds. Hasson, D. and Dickmann, A. National Council for Research and Development, 1975.

18. Tabor, H. The promise of solar ponds, *Kidma*, 5(3), 8-11, 1980.

19. Chemicals Bloom in the Desert, *Chemical Week*, Feb. 1979.

20. Forti, M. Experiments in Jojoba cultivation in 1977. Research and Development Authority, Ben Gurion Univ. of the Negev. October 1978 (Mimeograph).

21. Underexploited Tropical plants with promising economic value. National Academy of Sciences, Washington, D.C. 1975.

22. Johnson, J.D. and Hinman, T.W. Oil and Rubber from Arid Land Plants. *Science*, 208-460, 1980.

23. Myers, N. New foods and innovative agriculture. Presented in the 'Right for food' conference, Concordia Univ., Montreal, May 1984.

24. Forti, M. Introduction of fodder shrubs and their evaluation for use in semi-arid areas of the north-western Negev. Publication of the Negev Institute for Arid Zone Research, Beer Sheva, Israel, 1971.

25. Schlechter, Y. (Ed.) The Negev — A desert reclaimed. United Nations Conference on desertification. Aug. 29 to Sept. 9., 1977. A/CONF. 74/20 (Mimeographed).

26. De Kock, G.C. Drought-resistant fodder shrub crops in South Africa, International Livestock Centre for Africa, Addis Ababa, Ethiopia, 1983.

27. Heth, D. and Dan, J. New Data on tree introduction in the Negev. Agricultural Research Organization, Leaflet No 65, Div. of Scientific Publications, Bet Dagan, Israel, 1978.
28. Heden, C.G. Phytotechnology in an information society. IFIAS Workshop, Sussex University. April 15-17, 1985.
29. Redenbaugh, K., Nichol, J., Kossler, M.E. and Paash. Encapsulation of somatic embryos for artificial seed production. *Ann. Meeting Reports*. In vitro 20/3, Part II, March 1984.
30. Gale, J. Controlled environment agriculture for hot desert region. In: *Plants and their atmospheric environment*. Grace, J., Ford, E.D. and Jarvis, P.G. (Eds.). The 21st Symposium of the British Ecological Society. Edinburgh, March 1979.
31. Bassham, J.A. Increasing crop production through more controlled photosynthesis. *Science* 197, 630-638, 1977.
32. Richmond, A. Spirulina. In: *Handbook for micro-algal mass cultures*. A.Richmond (Ed.) CRC Press, Roca Raton, Florida 1986.
33. Richmond, A. Phototropic Microalgae. In: Rehm, H.J. and Reed, G. (eds.) *Biotechnology* 3, 110-143. Verlag Chemie, Weinheim, 1983.
34. Becker, E.W. Nutritional properties of microalgaes: potentials and constraints. In: *Handbook of micro-algal mass cultures*. A.Richmond (ed.), CRC Press, Roca Raton, Florida 1986.
35. Hernandez, V., Gross, U. and Gross, R. Some remarks about a testing program for single cell protein (SCP) as food additives in Peru, on the example of the microalgae *Scenedesmus acutus*, Institudo de nutricion, Tr. Tizon, Y. Bue nop, 276 Lima, 11 Peru.
36. Ben-Amotz, A. and Avron, M. On the mechanism of osmoregulation in Dunaliella. In: *Energetics and Structure of Halophilic Microorganisms*, Caplan, S.R. and Ginzburg (eds.), 523-541, Elsevier, Amsterdam, 1978.
37. Granoth, G. and Porath, D. An attempt to optimize feed utilization by Tilapia in a flow-through aquaculture. In: *Proceeding International Symp.* on *Tilapia and aquaculture*. Fishelzon, E. (ed.), 550-558, Natzareth, Israel, 1983.
38. Oron, G., Granoth, G. and Porath, D. Intensified controlled fish growth in tanks implementing a multipurpose flow device. *Biotechnology and bioengineering*, 25, 351-361, 1983.
39. Prof. R. Yagil, private communication, 1985. Faculty of Medicine, Ben-Gurion Univ., Beer-Sheva, Israel.

Comments on <u>Greening of the Desert</u>

Prof. Dr. E. El-Hinnawi
National Research Centre, Cairo, Egypt

Although this overview is well written, it tries to cover several issues at the same time. It would have been much better if the author had confined himself to the subject of 'Greening the Desert' per se.

Several statements in the paper need further justification and/or referencing. For example:

1. The author mentions that 'Humanity by the next century will have rid itself from the present burden of dependence on fossil fuel.' This is not true. Dependence on fossil fuels will continue in the far future, although it will decrease. Studies of IIASA, United Nations, etc. have clearly indicated that fossil fuels will continue to be the main source of energy for hundreds of years.

2. The author mentions that, 'It is the obligation of the more prosperous people living in the more humid, highly productive regions to assist their fellow human beings, natives of the dry lands.. etc.' This is again not true and there is no justification for such statements. First, not all people living in humid areas are more prosperous than those living in arid areas. Second, not all humid areas are highly productive. Third, it is the obligation of governments themselves to take the necessary measures to 'green the deserts' through appropriate planning.

3. The author states 'Greening of the desert obviously has also political ramifications, for the deprivation prevailing today in the drylands could in the long run threaten world peace.' This a strong statement. It is true that migration of people after the drought has caused some border problems between African countries, for example, but such problems were strictly localized and regional. The magnitude of such conflicts cannot threaten the world peace.

The author draws heavily on examples from Israel. This is understandable since he is working at the Ben Gurion University. But since the paper is an overview on the subject, it should be 'internationalized.' There are several examples and success stories of greening the deserts in China, Arab countries, African countries, Australia, USA, etc. I would have liked to see a critical evaluation of such experiences, with particular reference to technologies used and, more important, of the socio-economic and environmental aspects of such undertakings.

There is a great deal of work carried out on the assessment of greening the desert, and the author should refer to publications of the United Nations Environment Program, World Watch Institute (New York), United Nations University, etc.

I would like also to draw the attention of the author to the annual State of the Environment Report for 1985 published by UNEP since it contains an update on genetic engineering with reference to tolerant crops for arid areas. Also of direct relevance to this paper is my booklet on 'Environmental Refugees' published by UNEP in 1985.

In conclusion, a revised version of this paper will be of great value in flagging an issue that is indeed very important for many developing countries.

Prof. Malcolm Slesser
Resource Use Institute, Scotland

'Is the greening of the desert economically feasible?' asks the author at the end of his essay. His answer is to say: 'Based on learned intuition, the various schemes and tactics described here represent in principle economically sound targets.' The purpose of this commentary is to look further into this optimism.

The author makes a convincing case of the desirability and the attractiveness of greening of the deserts. The technologies he describes are workable. In other words, technologically, scientifically, socially and environmentally speaking his proposals are sound, and no further comment is needed. But will most of them come about?

Amos Richmond points out that '...desert-like conditions are expanding at an alarming rate.' From this observation we may conclude that in those areas no natural market forces are hastening to bring in the technologies described in the paper. Quite the reverse. Thus their economic potential has yet to be recognized or evaluated. What is the stumbling block?

It is energy.

The author implies this in a couple of comments. 'No method, however, has yet been invented that would desalinate seawater at a cost that is not totally prohibitive for agricultural production,' and '...Reverse osmosis is the desalination process with the lowest energy requirement...'

Indeed, Amos Richmond notes in the third paragraph of the paper that 'Humanity...will have rid itself from the present burden of dependence on fossil fuels, and will be producing abundant energy from essentially unlimited resources.' If he is right, and if in addition, these unlimited resources reflect cheap energy, then the prospects are indeed good, and I would accept that many of the technologies he discusses will come to pass. There will, of course, always be a trade-off, even if energy were to be cheap, between competing options. One of the pressures for using the desert lands will undoubtedly be the need of growing populations. Then the question will arise whether the additional food may not be more economically grown by further intensification of existing humid croplands. My own impression from examining the energetics of dryland farming is that the energy requirement of water provision will tend to militate against dryland farming.

However this reflects simply the economic aspects of the question. The social and environmental reasons suggest that considerable effort should go into dryland crop raising, even if it be but pasture or desert shrubs, such as Jojoba or Guayule. The economics of the matter may be of the least importance. But having said that we have to recognize that such an approach is only open to a rich country, not a poor one, just in the same way that most solar technology is too capital intensive to be used by any but rich countries.

My feeling is that it is a mistake to hang the merits of these dryland techniques on their economic viability. Further, I disagree completely with Amos Richmond's optimism that we shall be 'producing abundant energy from essentially unlimited resources,' if by this statement he implies cheap energy. While I do not see any emerging energy crisis, the long-term growth in energy supply will be slow, slower perhaps than population growth. The fraction of world capitalization devoted to the energy sector will steadily rise, thereby restricting that available for other purposes.

In conclusion I accept and applaud the social, environmental and technological basis of Amos Richmond's argument. I seriously question whether many of these technologies will be introduced on economic grounds. The greening of the desert may turn out to be a matter of policy, not economics.

Responses to Comments on <u>Greening of the Desert</u>

Amos Richmond

1. *Bent Elbek*: I have no particular comment to make on his criticism. Regarding dependence on solar energy; in the past decade great progress was achieved in photovoltaics and the prospects for mass production of panels that convert solar irradiance directly into electricity seems not so remote any more. In any case, the idea to provide people with kerosene stoves does not seem practical. Give-away stoves is no problem perhaps, but organizing a network that distributes the kerosene regularly?

2. *Malcolm Slesser*: I agree that 'greening' of deserts represents an optimistic approach towards solving the problem of hunger, malnutrition and dire poverty in general. My basic thesis is that in the poverty-stricken lands, there are ways and means by which to improve a desperate situation which, if unattended, will go from bad to worse. If we are to exclude charity as a permanent solution, what other choice is there for the poor inhabitants of many arid lands but to seek solutions based on rational thinking and technology? Would the capital that would then have to be invested bear commercial interest? Certainly not at the start, but the long term effects of education and development are impossible to calculate.

Optimism is indeed needed to hope that people will eventually take a path that, with proper aid, will bring relief and improve their lot. Conviction is needed to believe in the importance of such a mission.

Of course, from a purely economic standpoint, nothing is certain in the ambition to 'green' arid lands. Clearly, economic considerations cannot form the driving force to start with such an endeavor.

3. *Essam El-Hinnawi:* I agree that at least one weakness of my paper is that it is based mostly on examples from Israel, with which I am most familiar. It is certainly true that there are several examples and success stories of 'greening the desert' in many countries, including of course, many Arab countries. Mention of this has been added to the text.

Regarding man's dependence on fossil fuels in the future: I have modified in the text the original statement which was, indeed, too extreme. Nevertheless, it is clear to me that the statement made by the critic, to wit: '. . . fossil fuels continuing to be the main sources of energy for hundreds of years to come . . .' seems to me meaningless. Could anybody, even a learned committee, in the 16th or 17th centuries predict the course of economic events and feasibilities in our time? And what about the pace of scientific achievements and technical developments which has been accelerating constantly?

Thus I propose that my perhaps naive optimism is yet better founded than Prof. El-Hinnawi's stark pessimism in this matter.

What Happened to the Energy Crisis? A Comment on the Global Commentary Papers

Bent Elbek
Niels Bohr Institute
University of Copenhagen

The papers in the 'Commentary' treat very different subjects. Nevertheless there are some common denominators. One is obviously the plight of the developing countries. Another is energy.

At the time of writing (January 1986, dating one's comments could be important) international oil prices are lower than they have been for more than a decade. The specter of the energy crisis has faded away. But it could reappear, because nothing fundamental has changed in the energy outlook. Oil is still the world's most important fuel. Its share of the primary energy supply has been reduced only slightly from 44% in 1975 to 40% in 1984. The world today consumes more oil than in 1973 drawing on the same limited resources. The main change since then is that the OPEC countries produce much less and non-OPEC countries much more. The United Kingdom, Mexico and the Soviet Union are the major new suppliers which, for the time being, have forced the OPEC countries to produce less than they can and want to. This is the basic fact behind today's falling oil prices. But the OPEC countries still possess about 75% of the proven oil reserves. It seems inevitable that sometime in a not too distant future the scene will be set for another oil crisis.

Tropical forests are in jeopardy mainly because they are used — and very inefficiently — as a source of fuel. On a global scale fuelwood contributes only about 6% of all primary energy. But in Africa, Latin America and South Asia the fraction is much higher. A donation of a simple kerosene stove and a reasonable supply of kerosene at a nominal price to every household in the most threatened regions could turn out to be a better development aid than many current projects.

The *heating up of the climate* is directly coupled to the massive use of fossil fuel in industrialized countries. Here a substitution of coal for oil, as it happened in the USA and some European countries, is certainly a step in the wrong direction. The misguided opposition to nuclear power is to a large extent responsible for this unfortunate development. Nevertheless nuclear power consumption has been growing at a substantial rate of 16% p.a. during the last decade, and could still contribute significantly to a reduction of the CO_2 emissions.

It is conceivable, that a better understanding of the greenhouse effect might lead to international restrictions on especially coal combustion everywhere. In this connection it should be remembered, that the communist countries, partly because of inefficient use, burn more than 50% of the world's coal. An effort to reduce CO_2 emissions therefore necessarily must include these countries. Negotiations on this subject could be at least as difficult as the arms reduction talks in Geneva.

The *greening of the desert* opens beautiful vistas. It is hard to judge the realism of the many interesting suggestions in the paper. However, the prophecy of abundant energy from unlimited resources is not supported by any of the numerous studies of future energy supplies which have been performed during the last ten years. In general one should be cautious of projects which depend on extensive use of solar energy. The technical and not least, the economical obstacles have in most cases been found to be formidable.

Urbanization in the industrialized world has been an energy intensive process. There is little reason to doubt that *urbanization in the developing countries* will be energy intensive too. In the terms of the paper, this makes the large cities vulnerable (as evidenced by strikes on public transport systems or power failures), but not necessarily to an unacceptable extent. If the cities are to develop into something better than vast slums, electrification is essential. Small industries or handicrafts can develop and living conditions in even the poorest households be vastly improved. The household consumption of electricity in today's developing cities is very low, around 150 kwh per household per year. This is about 5% of the household consumption in an industrialized country. What would be a reasonable consumption in a developing country? Electric light, a radio or TV-set, an electric fan and a small refrigerator sound modest enough. This however, would require about 800 kwh per household per year. For a 10 million city about 3 TWh per year or the output of a large power station. Add to this industrial and commercial uses of electricity, and the need for a significant generating capacity becomes clear. If hydropower is not available, nuclear power seems the obvious solution, if such demands are to be met in an environmentally acceptable way. Indeed, the high population density in a city would make the electric grid compact, relatively cheap and a suitable load for a nuclear plant. The paper's reflection on hypothetical exposures to low level radiation and other risks has little relevance when the huge benefits of even a modest supply of electricity are considered.

The paper on the *global debt problem* makes it abundantly clear, that there are numerous connections between the energy problem and the debt problem. Today some oil producing countries as Mexico and Nigeria are deeply in debt and the current balance of the OPEC-group has been negative since 1982.

The low oil prices of today will certainly aggravate the debt problem of the oil producing developing countries. On the other hand, the far greater group of oil-importing developing countries can foresee a relief, which is also the case for most of the industrialized countries. Especially Japan will strengthen its already very strong position.

For a long time one has ascribed most of the economic ills of the world to the high oil prices. Now, when prices are going down, a new set of problems appears. Yet there is the hope that the process to some extent is reversible and that a new splurge of economic activity might help to solve the debt problem. But in all probability the energy problem has only disappeared temporarily. The basic situation is only marginally different from that of 1973 and 1979. The need for energy in the developing countries is forever growing and in the industrialized countries the public awareness of environmental problems has restricted the number of options available. It will require political skill and good luck if we are not going to reenact the energy crisis sometime in the 1990s.

About the IFIAS

The International Federation of Institutes for Advanced Study is an association of 35 leading research institutes which collaborate to address major global problems of long-term importance in environment, economy and science and technology. IFIAS research programs are interdisciplinary, seeking to advance understanding of complex systems for the improved management in a rapidly changing world with an uncertain future. IFIAS stands for the more effective and consistent use of scientific understanding in world councils, and for the adoption of long-term strategic thinking.

IFIAS Executive Committee Members

Sir Hermann Bondi   Chairman
Master, Churchill College
Cambridge, England

Prof. Darcy F. de Almeida   Vice Chairman
Instituto de Biofisica
Rio de Janeiro, Brazil

Dr. Thomas R. Odhiambo
International Centre of
Insect Physiology & Ecology
Nairobi, Kenya

Prof. C. H. Geoff Oldham
Science Policy Research Unit
Brighton, England

Mr. J. Egbert Prins
Delft Hydraulics
Delft, The Netherlands

Dr. Ian Burton   Director, IFIAS
IFIAS Secretariat
Toronto, Canada

IFIAS Member Institutes

Athens Center of Ekistics
Athens 10210
Greece

Center for Remote Sensing
Boston University
Boston, Mass. 02215
USA

Centro de Investigacion y de
Estudios Avanzados del IPN
(CINVESTAV)
07000 Mexico D.F.
Mexico

El Colegio de Mexico A.C.
01000 Mexico D.F.
Mexico

Delft Hydraulics
2600 MH Delft
The Netherlands

Food Research Institute
Stanford University
Stanford, CA 94305
USA

Global Studies Center
Arlington, VA 22209
USA

Graduate Institute of
International Studies
CH-1211 Geneva 21
Switzerland

Institut National de la
Recherche Scientifique
University of Quebec
Sainte-Foy, Quebec G1V 4C7
Canada

Institute for
Environmental Studies
University of Toronto
Toronto, Ontario M5S 1A4

Institute for European
Environmental Policy
D-5300 Bonn 1
West Germany

Institute for Futures Studies
DK-1468 Copenhagen K
Denmark

Institute for Studies on Research
and Scientific Documentation
00100 Rome
Italy

Institute for World Economics of the
Hungarian Academy of Sciences
(IWEHAS)
H-1531 Budapest
Hungary

Instituto de Biofisica
UFRJ - CCS - Cidade Universitaria
21941 - Rio de Janeiro - RJ
Brazil

Instituto Brasileiro de Economia
20.000 - Rio de Janeiro - RJ
Brazil

Instituto de Ciencias del Hombre (ICH)
28001 Madrid
Spain

Instituts Internationaux de
Physique et de Chimie
(Solvay Institute)
B-1050 Brussels
Belgium

International Centre of Insect
Physiology and Ecology (ICIPE)
Nairobi
Kenya

International Centre for
Theoretical Physics (ICTP)
34100 Trieste
Italy

The Jacob Blaustein Institute
for Desert Research
Ben-Gurion University of the Negev
Israel 84990

The Japan Economic Research
Center (JERC)
Tokyo 100
Japan

Kernforschungsanlage Jülich GmbH
D-5170 Jülich
West Germany

Marga Institute
Colombo 5
Sri Lanka

National Institute for Research
Advancement (NIRA)
Tokyo 160
Japan

National Research Center for Science
and Technology for Development
(NRCSTD)
Beijing
People's Republic of China

National Research Centre
Dokki-Cairo
Egypt

Niels Bohr Institute
2100 Copenhagen
Denmark

Research Institute
King Fahd University of
Petroleum and Minerals
Dhahran 31261
Saudi Arabia

Research Policy Institute
University of Lund
S-220 02 Lund
Sweden

Royal Scientific Society
Amman
Jordan

Science Policy Research
Unit (SPRU)
University of Sussex
Brighton BN1 9RF
England

Tata Institute of Fundamental Research
Bombay 400 005
India

University Corporation for
Atmospheric Research (UCAR)
Boulder, Col. 80307-3000
USA

The Weizmann Institute of Science
Rehovot 76100
Israel

Winrock International Institute
for Agricultural Development
Morrilton, Ark. 72110
USA

Woods Hole Oceanographic Institution
(WHOI)
Woods Hole, Mass. 02543
USA

World Resources Institute
Washington, DC 20006
USA

IFIAS Corporate Affiliates

AKZO NV
Arnhem, The Netherlands

ATLAS COPCO AB
Stockholm, Sweden

**DSM CORPORATE PLANNING
AND DEVELOPMENT**
Heerlen, The Netherlands

ENEA
Rome, Italy

GIST-BROCADES
Delft, The Netherlands

OCE-VAN DER GRINTEN
Venlo, The Netherlands

PHILLIPS INTERNATIONAL
Eindhoven, The Netherlands

SHELL INTERNATIONAL PETROLEUM MIJ.
Den Haag, The Netherlands

SKANDINAVISKA ENSKILDA BANKEN
Stockholm, Sweden

UNILEVER RESEARCH LABORATORIUM
Vlaardingen, The Netherlands

VBB AB
Stockholm, Sweden

VOLKER STEVIN WEGEN EN ASFALT
Utrecht, The Netherlands